W9-AZU-760

STORIES OF

*Favorite Operas*

by *Clyde Robert Bulla*

BIZET PUCCINI ROSSINI

# STORIES OF
# *Favorite Operas*

*by* CLYDE ROBERT BULLA

*Illustrations by Robert Galster*

782.1
B

THOMAS Y. CROWELL COMPANY

NEW YORK

60-9611

Copyright © 1959 by Clyde Robert Bulla.
All rights reserved. No part of this book
may be reproduced in any form, except by a reviewer,
without the permission of the publisher.
Manufactured in the United States of America
Library of Congress Catalog No. 59-11389
First Printing

TO *Eugene,*
*who looks forward, along with me,*
*to each new opera season*

# INTRODUCTORY NOTE

OPERA STORIES come from many places and many periods in history. Some are ancient legends; some are tales of the Middle Ages; others are from modern novels, short stories, and plays. Each has been rewritten and reshaped for the operatic stage. The story in its operatic form is called a libretto, an Italian word meaning "little book."

Sometimes a composer wrote his own librettos. More often they were written by others. Composers and librettists wrote for audiences of their own time and place. If popular taste ran to sentiment, operas of the day were sentimental. If audiences favored humor or violence or gloomy, complicated plots, those tastes were reflected in the operas of the period.

Among the operas we hear today are some of the world's great stories. Among them, too, are plots that seem overdone and old-fashioned to us now. Because of their music they are kept alive. Because of their music we can still find in them excitement and beauty and meaning.

# CONTENTS

# The Marriage of Figaro

In 1784 the French playwright Beaumarchais produced his play *The Marriage of Figaro* in Paris. It carried on the story he had begun in an earlier comedy, *The Barber of Seville*.

In the summer of 1785 the new play was suggested to Wolfgang Mozart as the subject of an opera. At that time the composer was living in Vienna, and his *Marriage of Figaro* was first performed there on May 1, 1786.

The time of the story is the late eighteenth century. The scene is the castle of the Count and Countess Almaviva near Seville.

As the curtain rises, Figaro, the count's servant, is measuring the floor of a room. He is soon to marry Susanna, the countess' pretty young maid, and this room is to be theirs. Count Almaviva has given them a bed

1

as a wedding present, and Figaro is measuring to find the best place for it.

Susanna is trying on a hat in front of the mirror. She is not impressed by the count's generosity. She does not trust him, and she complains that he has been showing her far too much attention.

The countess rings for her, and she hurries away.

Figaro thinks over what Susanna has said. He considers himself more than a match for his master. He says to himself, "If the count wants to dance, I'll play the tune!"

He leaves, and Doctor Bartolo enters with his elderly housekeeper, Marcellina. The doctor was once the countess' guardian, and he hoped to marry her until Figaro interfered. Ever since he has waited to even the score with Figaro. Now his chance has come.

Marcellina is in love with Figaro. She has lent him money which he cannot repay. Because of this, she is trying to force him into marrying her. Doctor Bartolo is helping her. Before he leaves, he promises to do everything in his power to see that his old housekeeper marries Figaro.

Marcellina is still there when Susanna returns. They exchange insults, and the old woman flounces out.

Cherubino, the count's page, enters. He is a romantic boy, in love with every pretty face he sees. Just now he is in love with the countess.

He tells Susanna of his present trouble. The count found him alone with Barbarina, the gardener's daughter. "He was in a fury," says Cherubino. "He is going to send me away unless the countess can get me pardoned."

Susanna has a ribbon belonging to the countess. Cherubino seizes it and refuses to give it back, but in exchange for it he sings Susanna a song he has written about the pleasure and pain of love.

The count approaches. Cherubino is afraid of him and hides behind a chair.

Susanna tries to send the count away, but he insists on talking to her. "Meet me in the garden this evening," he says.

Before she can answer, they hear the voice of Basilio, the music master, who comes often to the castle. He is outside, looking for the count.

The count does not want to be found talking with Susanna. He steps behind the chair which was Cherubino's hiding place. The boy manages to keep out of his master's sight. He scrambles around the chair and sits in it, and Susanna hastily covers him with a dress.

The music master enters and asks for the count.

"What should I know about the count?" says Susanna coldly. "Go away."

But Basilio lingers, repeating the latest gossip. Some of it has to do with Cherubino.

"That song he was singing," he says. "Was it for you or the countess? You should see how he looks at her when he waits on her at the table. If the count should ever notice—"

The count is so jealous and indignant that he cannot restrain himself. He comes forward and orders Basilio to find that scoundrel Cherubino and drive him out of the castle.

"Poor boy," says Susanna. "Forgive him."

"Forgive him?" says the count. "I know more about him than you do." Yesterday, he says, the page was hiding in the room of Barbarina, the gardener's daughter. "I gently lifted the table cloth, and there he was," says the count. He shows them how it happened by lifting the dress from the chair.

To his amazement, he again uncovers Cherubino!

Basilio is gleeful. Susanna is ready to faint. The count threatens to send for Figaro so that he can witness the girl's unfaithfulness.

"Send for him," says Susanna defiantly. "I've nothing to hide." She explains that Cherubino came to tell her the count was angry with him. The boy only wanted her to ask the countess to speak a word in his favor. "When you came in," she says, "we were both confused, and he hid behind the chair."

"Then he heard every word I said to you!" says the count.

"I tried my best *not* to hear," says Cherubino.

A group of peasants enters, followed by Figaro. The peasants sing in praise of the count, and Figaro asks him to place the wedding veil on Susanna's head.

The count is secretly trying to delay the wedding. He answers that he will perform the ceremony at a more suitable time.

Cherubino has taken no part in the rejoicing.

"Poor boy," says Susanna. "He is unhappy because he has been dismissed from the castle."

Cherubino asks the count's forgiveness.

"You don't deserve it," says the count, "but you shall be pardoned. I'll do still more. There is a vacant place in my regiment. I give it to you, and you shall leave at once for the army."

Figaro bids Cherubino good-by and tells him he will find the army far different from the carefree life he has known.

The scene of Act II is the countess' room. The countess is alone, sadly reflecting that the count no longer loves her. She knows of his attentions to Susanna.

Susanna enters. Figaro follows and tells the countess not to be anxious. He can always be depended on for an idea, and he unfolds his latest one. He has just sent Basilio to the count with an anonymous letter. The letter informs the count that the countess is going to meet a man in the garden tonight.

"Oh, heavens!" cries the countess. "How could you, when the count is so jealous!"

"So much the better," says Figaro. "Then he may realize his game is one that others can play. He will spend the day worrying about you. In the meantime, Susanna and I will be married, and he will be too busy to interfere."

He has still another idea for keeping the count occupied. He tells Susanna, "Let him know that you will meet him in the garden this evening."

Susanna answers that she has no intention of meeting the count in the garden.

"No, we'll have Cherubino dressed as a woman and send him to keep your appointment," says Figaro. Then the countess will arrive and catch the count. After that he will be obliged to grant her anything she wishes!

He leaves, delighted with the complications he is piling up.

Cherubino enters. Susanna locks the door, and she and the countess dress him as a woman. While Susanna is in an alcove, looking for some ribbon, the count knocks. "Why is the door locked?" he shouts.

Cherubino runs into the dressing room and hides.

The countess unlocks the door for the count. She explains that she locked it only because she was trying on a dress. "There was no one here but Susanna. She has gone to her own room."

"Something certainly seems to have disturbed you," he says, and he shows her a letter. It is the anonymous letter written by Figaro.

There is a noise in the dressing room.

"There's someone in there," says the count.

"It's Susanna," says the countess.

"You told me she had gone to her own room," says the count.

"Either her room or mine," says the countess. "I didn't notice."

While the count shouts for Susanna to come out of the dressing room, the frightened girl is peeping out of the alcove in the back.

The count loses patience. Since his wife will not unlock the dressing-room door, he will have it forced.

He wants no scandal in front of the servants, so he decides to force the lock himself. He goes to find the tools he will need. He takes the countess with him so that she cannot release whoever is in the dressing room, and he locks the outside door behind them.

Susanna leaves the alcove. She tells Cherubino to come out and be quick.

The boy unlocks the dressing-room door and comes out. He looks desperately about. The only escape is through the window. It is a long drop to the ground, but he jumps.

Susanna takes his place in the dressing room. The

count and countess return. He is sure everything is just as he left it. He gives the countess her choice of opening the dressing-room door or standing by while he forces the lock.

The countess confesses. Susanna is not in the dressing room, she says. It is only poor little Cherubino.

"Must I find that imp everywhere I go!" cries the count.

He opens the door. Both he and the countess are astonished at the sight of Susanna.

"There's trickery here!" he exclaims. He searches in the dressing room, still expecting to find Cherubino.

While he is out of hearing, Susanna tells the countess that the boy has escaped.

The bewildered count comes out. "Then Cherubino is not here?" he says.

"I told you that only to tease you," says the countess.

The count brings up the matter of the anonymous letter. Susanna and the countess tell him it was only some of Figaro's foolishness.

Figaro comes in to announce that it is time for him and Susanna to go to the church for their wedding.

The count still hopes to delay the wedding. Playing for time, he confronts Figaro with the anonymous letter.

At first Figaro denies that he knows anything about it. Susanna and the countess make him understand that they have given away the secret. They try to make it appear as nothing more than a harmless joke, and at last he admits his part in it.

He and Susanna and the countess appeal to the count not to delay the marriage any longer.

But there is another delay. Antonio, the gardener, enters, complaining about the people who throw things out the windows into his flower beds. Today is the worst yet—someone has thrown out a man.

The count asks, "This man—where is he?"

"He ran away," says Antonio.

Again the count is suspicious.

"You must help us," Susanna whispers to Figaro. "It was Cherubino."

"What a fuss over nothing!" Figaro says to the count. "If you want to know who jumped out the window, it was I!"

The count does not believe him. Neither does the gardener. The man who jumped was hardly half the size of Figaro, he says. He suspects it was Cherubino.

"Cherubino left today for Seville," says Figaro.

"If you jumped out the window," says the count, "tell me why."

"I was in there waiting for Susanna, when I heard your voice," says Figaro. "You sounded so angry, I thought you knew I had written the anonymous letter. I was afraid, so I jumped out the window."

"Then this paper I picked up must be yours," says the gardener.

The count seizes the paper. It is Cherubino's army commission.

He gazes at Figaro and waits for an explanation.

"The boy left his commission with me before he went away," says Figaro.

"What for?" asks the count.

"I was going to have it sealed for him," answers Figaro.

The count sees that, through some oversight, the commission has *not* been sealed. In exasperation, he tears up the paper.

Figaro is congratulating himself on his cleverness, when a new complication arises.

Basilio, Doctor Bartolo, and Marcellina arrive. The two men are representing the old woman, who demands her legal rights. Figaro has borrowed from her on condition that he would marry her if he could not repay the money.

Figaro is trapped. Susanna and the countess are thrown into confusion. Marcellina and her two advisers call for justice, and the count is pleased at the turn of affairs.

Act III takes place in a hall in the castle. The count is there, wracking his brain over the strange happenings of the day. He wonders who jumped out the window—

was it really Figaro? And did Cherubino really go to Seville?—he has sent Basilio to find out.

While his back is turned, the countess brings Susanna into the hall, then slips away. Susanna speaks to the count. He asks her again to meet him in the garden. This time she pretends to agree.

Figaro comes into the hall and takes Susanna away.

The count watches them go. In a burst of resentment, he asks himself why he should give up Susanna to this low-born servant.

"I am master," he declares, "and he shall laugh at me and defy me no longer!"

Marcellina, Doctor Bartolo, and Figaro come in. Curzio, a lawyer, is with them.

Curzio reports what the court has decided. Figaro must either pay Marcellina or marry her.

She has lent him so much money that paying her seems out of the question. But Figaro flatly refuses to marry the old woman. "I am of noble birth," he says, "and therefore I cannot marry without my parents' consent."

The count is contemptuous. "Who are your parents and where are they?" he asks.

Figaro does not know. He was stolen from his parents when he was a baby. The robbers who carried him away found him dressed in jewels and fine linen. This is proof enough of his high station. Besides, he has a curious mark on his arm that might some day identify him.

Marcellina has been listening intently. She asks in great excitement, "A mark in the shape of a spatula?"

"How did you know?" asks Figaro.

"It is he!" she cries. Figaro is her own son, and Doctor Bartolo is his father.

Susanna enters, bringing the money she has raised to pay Figaro's debt.

"You are too late," the lawyer tells her. "The case is settled."

Susanna sees Marcellina in Figaro's arms. "He's false to me!" she cries, and she boxes Figaro's ears.

But once she understands the situation, she rejoices along with Figaro and his new-found parents. The count, leaving with the lawyer, mutters darkly that their joy will not last long.

Figaro is showered with wedding gifts. Marcellina cancels his debt to her. Susanna gives him the purse of money she has raised. Doctor Bartolo gives him still another purse, and the two happy couples go away together.

Cherubino enters with Barbarina, the gardener's daughter. She has invited him to her home where, she says, he will meet all the prettiest girls in the village.

"What if the count should follow me?" asks Cherubino. "He thinks I have gone to Seville."

Barbarina tells him she will dress him as a girl. Then he will not be recognized.

They hurry away.

The countess enters. Once more she sadly remembers the days when the count was faithful to her. As she leaves, she expresses the hope that some day they may be happy together again.

The count and the gardener come through the hall. The gardener is telling his master that Cherubino has not gone to Seville.

"Here is his hat to prove what I say," he says. "Not only that, he has been at my house today dressed as a girl."

The two men go in search of Cherubino.

Now the countess and Susanna come into the hall. Susanna says she has spoken to the count and promised to meet him in the garden.

The countess wants the appointment made more definite. "Write to him," she says.

She dictates, while Susanna writes. They seal the letter with a pin and add a note asking the count to send back the pin as an answer.

Barbarina enters with a group of peasant girls. Cherubino is with them, dressed as a girl. They have brought flowers to the countess. She does not recognize Cherubino, but she is charmed by his prettiness.

"Come and give me your flowers," she says.

At that moment the count and the gardener enter. The gardener pulls off Cherubino's headdress and replaces it with his soldier's hat.

Barbarina pleads for Cherubino and asks the count to give her the boy as her little husband.

Figaro comes in and says it is time to start the dancing.

The count tells him maliciously that Cherubino has confessed. It was the boy who jumped out the window this morning.

"That may be true," answers Figaro. "If I could make the jump, surely the boy could do the same thing."

He and Susanna and the wedding guests form a procession and march before the count and countess. Susanna kneels before the count. As he places the bridal veil on her head, she gives him the letter she has written.

Later, during the dancing, Figaro tells Susanna, "Someone has put a note into his lordship's hand. It must have been sealed with a pin, because he has pricked his finger!"

The count makes a speech. The celebration will continue into the night, he says, with singing, dancing, feasting, and fireworks.

When Act IV begins, it is night. Barbarina is alone in the garden. The count has given her the pin to return to Susanna, and Barbarina has lost it. She is searching for it by lantern light.

Marcellina and Figaro enter. Barbarina innocently tells them she has lost the pin the count gave her to take back to Susanna.

"To Susanna? The pin?" cries Figaro. Now he is sure Susanna has been deceiving him. After Barbarina leaves, he exclaims that all is lost, and he stalks out of the garden.

Now that Marcellina need not be jealous of Susanna, she has grown fond of the girl. "I'm sure she is innocent," she tells herself. "Besides, women should defend one another." And she goes to tell Susanna what she has heard.

Barbarina comes back and goes into an arbor to wait for Cherubino. Figaro enters with Basilio and Doctor Bartolo. He has brought the two men to witness Susanna's treachery. Any minute now, he tells them, she will be here to meet the count.

He sends them into hiding. "When I whistle," he says, "you come out together."

He leaves. Basilio sighs over the follies of youth, but he admits that he was once as foolish as Figaro.

After the men have hidden themselves, Figaro returns to watch for Susanna.

The countess and Susanna come into the garden. They are disguised in each other's dresses. Marcellina has come with them so that she may see the outcome of the plot. She steps into one of the arbors.

By this time Susanna knows that Figaro is watching and listening in the darkness. She mischievously pretends to be waiting for the count with great longing.

"Shameless!" mutters Figaro.

Cherubino comes to find Barbarina. In the darkness he sees the countess and mistakes her for Susanna. He asks her for a kiss. Embarrassed, she tries to draw away.

The count enters. He, too, mistakes his wife for Susanna.

Cherubino tries to kiss the countess. The count steps between them, and Cherubino kisses him by mistake.

In a panic, the boy darts into the nearest arbor. Meanwhile, Figaro has come forward. The count aims a blow at Cherubino and strikes Figaro instead.

Figaro goes back into hiding. The count is left with the countess. Still thinking she is Susanna, he takes her hand and they go away together.

Figaro starts after them. Susanna calls him back. She tries to disguise her voice as the countess', but he recognizes her.

Addressing her as the countess, he says dramatically, "I kneel at your feet! I am trembling with devotion! Give me your hand."

Angrily she gives him a box on the ear.

He tells her then that he knew she was not the countess. She tells him she only wanted to punish him for doubting her.

As they go into an arbor together, the count returns. He still thinks Susanna is the countess, and it appears to him that Figaro is forcing his attentions on her. Furiously he orders Figaro seized.

Doctor Bartolo, Basilio, Curzio, and a crowd of servants come forward.

The count goes into the arbor where he supposes his wife is hiding. He brings out first Cherubino, then Barbarina, Marcellina, and Susanna.

"Forgive me!" says Susanna.

The count, believing her to be his wife, replies, "No, I renounce you!"

The countess comes from the other side of the garden and reveals herself. The count is crushed. He begs his wife's forgiveness. She gladly pardons him, and the opera ends happily for all.

# Don Giovanni

In January, 1787, Mozart visited Prague, where his *Marriage of Figaro* was the success of the season. In February he returned home to Vienna with a commission to write a new opera for the Prague company.

He was soon at work on *Don Giovanni*. The story was based on a seventeenth-century Spanish play, *The Mocker of Seville and the Stone Guest*.

Mozart went back to Prague in September. There in the country home of a friend he finished the opera. It was first performed in Prague on October 29, 1787.

*Don Giovanni* is the story of a dissolute Spanish nobleman who spends his life seeking pleasure. As the opera opens, he is in the midst of his latest amorous adventure. He has stolen into the house of Donna Anna, daughter of the commandant of Seville.

His servant, Leporello, is keeping watch outside.

Walking up and down in the darkness, he complains that he is weary of serving such a master.

At the sound of footsteps, he hides himself.

Don Giovanni and Donna Anna come out of the house. At first she had mistaken him for her lover, Don Ottavio. Then she discovered he was a stranger. Indignantly she demanded his name.

Now Don Giovanni wishes to escape, but Donna Anna is clutching his arm and calling for help. Her father hears her and comes out of the house. She runs back inside to summon more aid.

The commandant draws his sword. Don Giovanni has no wish to fight the old man, but he is forced to defend himself. They fight, and the commandant falls, mortally wounded.

Don Giovanni and Leporello fly from the scene.

Donna Anna returns with Don Ottavio. They find the body of the commandant.

Donna Anna is distracted with grief, and Don Ottavio pledges to avenge her father's death.

In the next scene it is early morning. Don Giovanni and Leporello are on a street in Seville. A lady approaches.

"At this distance she is beautiful," says Don Giovanni, and he and the servant step out of sight so that they may look at her more closely.

The lady is Donna Elvira. Once she was jilted by Don

Giovanni, and she fiercely pours out her feelings against the man who won her love and deserted her.

Don Giovanni does not even remember her.

"Poor little girl!" he says, and he speaks to her. She turns on him furiously. He recognizes her then.

In a long speech she accuses him of lies and faithlessness. Leporello admires the speech. It is just like a printed book, he says.

Don Giovanni tries to explain that he had important reasons for leaving her. "Since you won't believe me, let this honest fellow tell you," he says, bringing Leporello forward.

While the stammering servant is trying to think of something to say, Don Giovanni escapes.

"Which way has he gone?" cries Donna Elvira.

"Be glad he is gone," says Leporello. "You are not the first woman he has deceived, and you will not be the last. Look—in this book I keep the names of his sweethearts, in villages and towns and even foreign places. There are countesses and serving maids and country girls. Whether they are young and pretty or old and plain, he considers it his duty to make love to them all."

He leaves her. Donna Elvira vows that she will have vengeance. Now that she knows Don Giovanni for what he is, she no longer loves him, she despises him!

The next scene shows Don Giovanni and Leporello in a country village. They have arrived in time for the festival. Zerlina, a pretty village girl, is about to be married to a rustic young peasant, Masetto.

Don Giovanni takes a fancy to Zerlina. So that he may be alone with her, he tells Leporello to take all the others to his palace and give them refreshments and entertainment. Masetto does not want to leave. Don Giovanni makes a threatening gesture toward his sword. Only then does Masetto go with the others.

Don Giovanni tells Zerlina that she is much too good for this peasant. He asks her to marry him, instead.

As they start off together, Donna Elvira appears. She has followed him here, and she is thankful she has come in time to save the poor girl from his treachery.

"This traitor means to deceive you," she tells Zerlina. "Leave him now, while there is time!" and she leads the girl away.

This is surely his unlucky day, sighs Don Giovanni. Nothing goes as he wishes it. He sees Donna Anna and Don Ottavio coming toward him. The final blow, he thinks.

But they greet him as a friend. They are in trouble, they tell him. He answers that he is at their service, and he asks Donna Anna why she is dressed in mourning.

Donna Elvira returns. "Monster!" she cries. She tells Donna Anna and Don Ottavio that this man's promises are not to be trusted and his heart is as cold as stone.

Don Giovanni pretends that the lady has gone mad,

but her earnestness impresses Donna Anna and Don Ottavio. They cannot help believing her.

"I'll follow you through all the world, proclaiming you a traitor!" declares Donna Elvira, as she leaves.

"Poor creature, she needs someone to watch over her," says Don Giovanni, and he follows her.

Donna Anna gazes after him in horror. The tone of his voice as he spoke those parting words has betrayed him.

"Oh, heaven!" she cries. "That was the voice of my father's murderer."

It is hard for Don Ottavio to believe a nobleman guilty of such a crime. He resolves to follow Don Giovanni and learn the truth.

When he and Donna Anna are gone, Leporello returns. "This master of mine is a madman!" he exclaims. "See, there he comes, looking as indifferent as if nothing had ever happened."

Don Giovanni comes into sight and asks how things are going.

"They could hardly be worse," answers Leporello. He has taken the peasants to the palace, and while he was entertaining them, Donna Elvira and Zerlina burst in. As usual, Donna Elvira was scolding and raving, and Leporello led her outside and locked the door.

"Bravo!" says Don Giovanni, and he starts off to the party.

The scene changes to the palace garden. The villagers are there, sitting about on the grass.

Zerlina is trying to convince Masetto that what happened was not her fault.

"Don't speak to me!" he says. "On the eve of our wedding a stranger comes between us. It's too much for me to bear."

"His flattery turned my head for a moment," she says. "Now I've forgotten it. Beat me, if my fault is so great. Then let there be peace between us."

Masetto cannot stay angry. He forgives her.

Don Giovanni enters. He sends the peasants into the palace to continue their celebration, while he manages to detain Zerlina. Again he tries to make love to her, but this time Masetto has stayed behind and is listening.

Don Giovanni makes the best of the situation. He invites the two into the palace and graciously leads them away.

Three masked figures come into the garden. They are Donna Elvira, Donna Anna, and Don Ottavio.

Leporello sees them from the window. He points them out to his master.

"Invite them in," says Don Giovanni.

The three maskers whisper to one another, "That voice—surely he is the one we came here to find!"

The next scene is the palace ballroom. A dance has

just ended. Masetto is growing surly. Don Giovanni is becoming more and more attentive to Zerlina, and she is not discouraging him.

The three maskers enter. Don Giovanni welcomes them. Another dance begins, and he dances with Zerlina.

Masetto is angry. Leporello urges him to choose a partner. Masetto refuses, and Leporello jokingly tries to make the young peasant dance with him.

"Let me go!" shouts Masetto. He frees himself, and Leporello runs away.

In the confusion, Don Giovanni sweeps Zerlina out of the ballroom. The girl calls for help. Masetto and the three maskers rush to her aid.

Don Giovanni appears, dragging Leporello.

"Here is the scoundrel! I've caught him!" he says,

trying to make it appear that his servant has forced his attentions on Zerlina.

The maskers are not deceived. Don Ottavio draws a pistol. He and the two women take off their masks, and they denounce Don Giovanni. Zerlina and Masetto join them.

They warn Don Giovanni that he will pay for his sins, and he faces them with bold defiance.

Act II opens on a street near the home of Donna Elvira. It is evening. Don Giovanni has escaped from his pursuers, and he and Leporello are arguing. Leporello is determined to leave his master. Don Giovanni soothes his ruffled feelings with money.

Don Giovanni is now interested in Donna Elvira's pretty serving maid. He thinks she may be more likely to trust him if he pretends to be a servant, too, and he exchanges cloaks with Leporello.

Donna Elvira comes to the window. Don Giovanni has a plan for getting her out of the way. Standing behind Leporello, he declares his love for her.

She looks out into the night, sees Leporello in his master's cloak, and thinks Don Giovanni has come back to her. In spite of all that has gone before, she is ready to forgive him.

She leaves the window. He hides in the shadows. She comes out of the house and meets Leporello, whom she still thinks is Don Giovanni.

"Swear to me that you will never again deceive me,"
she says.

"I swear!" promises Leporello.

Don Giovanni shouts to frighten Donna Elvira. She
screams, and she and Leporello run out together.

Now Don Giovanni is free to serenade the maid. He
sings outside her window. Before she can answer, there
is an interruption. Masetto comes on the scene in com-

pany with several armed villagers. They are looking for Don Giovanni.

Posing as Leporello, Don Giovanni offers to help track down the wicked nobleman. He sends the villagers off in search of him.

When he and Masetto are alone, he asks the peasant if he is well armed. The gullible Masetto shows Don Giovanni his sword and pistol. Don Giovanni takes the sword, gives the peasant a beating with it, and runs away.

Zerlina comes looking for Masetto. She hears his groans and goes to help him. Comforting him, she says, "My love will make you well."

The scene changes to the dark courtyard before the house of Donna Anna. Leporello has come there with Donna Elvira. He is trying to escape before she discovers that he is not Don Giovanni.

Donna Anna enters with Don Ottavio. She is still mourning for her father, and Don Ottavio tries to console her.

As Leporello is about to slip out through a doorway, Zerlina and Masetto come by and seize him. They are sure they have captured Don Giovanni. Their shouts bring Donna Anna and Don Ottavio.

Shaking with fright, Leporello tells them he is only the servant. He begs them not to punish him for the sins of his wicked master, and at last he escapes.

Don Ottavio is more than ever convinced that it was Don Giovanni who murdered Donna Anna's father. He vows again that the villain will be punished.

The next scene is a moonlit churchyard. One of the monuments there is a statue of the commandant, Donna Anna's father.

Don Giovanni leaps over the wall. Leporello soon joins him.

Don Giovanni gives an account of his latest adventure. He met a beautiful young lady, but she recognized him and took fright. At her screams, people came running, and he leaped into the churchyard. He laughs heartily as he finishes the story.

A solemn voice speaks: "Your jest will turn to woe before the morning."

Don Giovanni sees the commandant's statue, and Leporello reads the inscription at the base of it: "Upon him who slew me, I wait here for vengeance."

The servant is seized with superstitious fear, but Don Giovanni says in cool amusement, "Tell the old man I invite him to supper."

Trembling, the servant obeys.

The statue slowly nods.

"Answer, if you can hear me," says Don Giovanni. "Will you come to supper?"

The statue answers in a strange, deep voice, "Yes!"

Leporello is faint with terror. Don Giovanni, still

unconcerned, remarks that this is truly a strange adventure. They must go, he says, to make ready for their stony guest.

The scene changes to a room in Donna Anna's house. Don Ottavio is asking the lady to put aside her grief and marry him.

She says reproachfully, "How can you speak so in this time of sadness?"

"Now I see you do not love me," he says.

She asks him not to doubt her. Her feelings for him have not changed.

The last scene is a hall in the palace of Don Giovanni. Guests have gathered. The table is set for a banquet.

Donna Elvira enters and pleads with Don Giovanni to change his evil ways. He only laughs at her.

She leaves. A moment later she screams. She rushes back into the hall and out through the opposite doorway.

Don Giovanni wonders what could have frightened her so. He sends Leporello to see.

The servant leaves, and he, too, cries out. He returns, pale and shaken. The statue is outside, he says. It has come to supper.

There is a heavy knock at the door. Leporello hides under the table. Don Giovanni throws open the door.

Slowly the statue enters. "I have been invited to supper," it says. "Behold me."

Don Giovanni takes the statue's hand. A deadly chill seizes him.

"You have time to repent," says the statue.

"I have no repentance!" says Don Giovanni.

The statue releases his hand and disappears. Flames rise about Don Giovanni. Voices from the underworld cry out that everlasting punishment awaits him. The flames rise higher, and Don Giovanni sinks out of sight.

Donna Elvira, Donna Anna, and Don Ottavio come into the hall. With them are Zerlina, Masetto, and a minister of justice. They have come to take Don Giovanni to prison.

Leporello tells them of his master's dreadful doom.

"Heaven has avenged us," says Don Ottavio.

Donna Anna promises him that they will be married, after a year of waiting. Donna Elvira tells them all that she will spend the rest of her days in a convent. Zerlina and Masetto plan to be married at once. As for Leporello, he declares that he will seek a better master and lead a better life.

# The Magic Flute

One of the most successful theater managers of his day was Emmanuel Schikaneder. In 1789 he became director of a theater in Vienna, and he called on Mozart for an opera. Popular taste at the time was for fantasy, comedy, and Oriental mysteries. The libretto Schikaneder provided was along these lines.

In the spring of 1791 Mozart was settled in a comfortable summerhouse on the theater grounds. There he worked on the opera, *The Magic Flute*. On September 30 of the same year it was first performed, with the composer conducting and Schikaneder singing the role of Papageno.

The opera quickly became popular. It was the last success Mozart was to know. In November he became ill. He died on December 5, 1791.

*The Magic Flute* takes place in ancient Egypt. The

first scene shows a rocky landscape. Tamino, a young prince, appears. He cries out for help from the serpent which is pursuing him, and falls unconscious.

Three ladies rush in with silver spears. They kill the serpent, then turn their attention to the young man. Never before have they seen anyone so handsome. Their queen must be told, they say. Perhaps this stranger can bring peace to her troubled heart.

They decide that one should stay to guard the young man. The other two will go to the queen. But they cannot agree on which one is to stay. They argue, and at last all three leave together.

Tamino regains consciousness and gazes at the dead serpent.

Someone is coming toward him. Half in alarm, he hides himself.

A strange figure enters—a man dressed in feathers. He is carrying a bird cage and playing a Panpipe. His name is Papageno, and he catches birds for the queen and her ladies. In return they give him wine, sugar bread, and figs. He is a cheerful fellow, although there are times when he is lonely and wishes for a pretty wife.

Tamino speaks to him, hoping to learn something about this strange land and the people who live here. As the prince draws near, Papageno grows frightened.

"Keep away from me," he says. "I am as strong as a giant."

"Then you must be the one who saved me from the serpent," says Tamino.

For the first time, the bird-catcher sees the dead serpent. He starts back in fright.

"How were you able to kill it without weapons?" asks the prince.

Papageno makes sure the serpent is dead. Then, boastfully, he answers that he had no need of a weapon. He killed the monster with one good squeeze of his hand.

The three ladies appear.

"Papageno!" they cry in menacing voices.

He wonders why they are angry. "Here, you lovely ladies," he says. He gives them his cage of birds and waits for the usual payment.

The first lady gives him a jug. "This time," she says, "the queen sends you water instead of wine."

The second lady gives him a stone instead of sugar bread.

The third lady, instead of giving him sweet figs, locks his mouth with a golden padlock.

This is the queen's punishment, they say, for telling lies to strangers and boasting of deeds done by others.

"We are the ones who killed the serpent," says one of the ladies. She gives the prince a miniature portrait. It is a picture of the queen's daughter. The queen has sent it to Tamino. "If you find it pleasing," says the lady, "happiness, honor, and glory await you."

The ladies go away. Shamed and embarrassed, Papageno leaves. Tamino gazes at the picture. Already he is in love with the princess, and he longs to see her and hold her in his arms.

The ladies return. They tell him that through her magic powers the queen knows his thoughts and has decided to make him completely happy.

There is a roll of thunder and a flash of lightning. The rocky cliff divides to reveal the Queen of the Night.

She steps down from her throne.

"Do not tremble," she says to Tamino, and she speaks to him of her daughter, Pamina. "My poor child is gone, carried off by an evil fiend. You are the one who shall set her free, and as your reward she shall be yours."

She steps back. Thunder crashes again, and the rocks close about her.

Tamino is not sure whether he is awake or dreaming. Papageno brings him back to reality. The bird-catcher has returned and is mumbling sadly as he points to the padlock on his mouth.

The three ladies appear with word that the queen has pardoned him. One of them removes the padlock. Papageno is overjoyed at being able to talk again, and he humbly promises to be more truthful in the future.

The ladies have brought Tamino a gift from the queen. It is a golden flute. They tell him of its great magical powers. A note on it will bring help in time of

danger, and its music will melt the coldest heart or bring joy in place of sadness.

Papageno asks if he may leave. No, say the ladies; the queen has a task for him. He must go with the prince to the temple of Sarastro.

Papageno asks to be excused. He has heard frightful tales of Sarastro's wickedness.

"Have no fear," say the ladies. "The prince will protect you." As further protection they give him a set of magic bells which he is to ring if danger threatens. The ladies leave, after promising the prince and Papageno that three spirits will come to guide them on their way.

The next scene is a luxurious room in Sarastro's palace. Monostatos, an evil Moor and a slave of Sarastro, comes in dragging Pamina. A prisoner there, she escaped and was overtaken by the Moor.

Slaves come forward and bind her with chains. She sinks unconscious upon a couch, and Monostatos sends the slaves away.

Papageno enters. He has lost his way and wandered into the palace. He sees the beautiful girl on the couch, and he pauses.

He and Monostatos catch sight of each other. Frightened out of their senses, they run in opposite directions.

Pamina revives. "Mother!" she cries.

Papageno comes back. He has recovered from his fright.

From her picture he recognizes Pamina as the daughter of the Queen of the Night. He offers to take her to the handsome prince who loves her and is on his way to set her free.

She says gratefully, "You have a tender heart."

That may be, sighs Papageno, but what good does it do him? Sometimes he feels like pulling out all his feathers when he thinks that Papageno has not yet found a Papagena to love.

She tells him to have patience, and they agree that love alone brings everlasting joy.

The next scene shows three temples in a grove. Tamino enters, guided by three spirits.

"Your journey is nearly ended," they tell him. "In the face of any danger, be steadfast, patient, and silent."

They leave him. He goes toward the temple on the right. A voice orders him back. He turns toward the temple on the left. Here, too, he is warned away.

Only the central temple remains. He approaches it, and the door opens. An old priest stands in the doorway.

Tamino asks if this is the realm of the hated Sarastro.

"You hate him?" asks the priest. "Tell me why."

Tamino answers that he has reason enough to hate the tyrant. Was it not Sarastro who took Pamina from her mother's arms and carried her away? He begs for word of the princess. Is she alive or dead?

"This I may not reveal," says the priest.

"When may I know?" asks Tamino.

"When the hand of friendship leads you to our sacred band," answers the priest, and he disappears into the temple.

Voices speak from within. They tell him Pamina is alive.

Filled with joy and gratitude, the prince begins to play the magic flute. From the distance comes an answer on Papageno's Panpipe.

Tamino hopes this is a signal that Papageno has found Pamina. He dashes off in the direction of the bird-catcher's music.

He is hardly out of sight when Papageno and Pamina enter. They are fleeing from the castle where the girl was a prisoner.

Again Papageno blows his Panpipe. Tamino answers on the flute to let them know that he is safe and nearby. They are hurrying to join him, when Monostatos springs up in their path. Slaves come forward with chains and rope.

Pamina and Papageno are in despair. Suddenly he remembers the bells given him by the three ladies. He takes them out and plays a tune.

They are magic bells, indeed. At the sound of the music, Monostatos and the slaves begin to sing and caper about in a ridiculous dance. Still singing, they dance away together.

Papageno and Pamina tell each other that if every honest man had bells like these he would have no enemies and his life would be one of perfect harmony.

Voices sing within the temple, praising Sarastro. Pamina and Papageno are alarmed. They fear they are lost if Sarastro is near.

Sarastro appears. Pamina throws herself on his mercy. She confesses that she has tried to run away, but only to escape the wicked Monostatos.

Sarastro answers her gently, although he refuses to set her free. It was for the sake of her own happiness that he took her from her mother, he says.

Monostatos enters bringing Tamino, whom he has just captured.

"It is he!" cries Pamina when she sees the prince.

"It is she!" cries Tamino. "It is not a dream!"

They fall into each other's arms.

Monostatos separates them. He tells Sarastro how Tamino and the bird-catcher have plotted Pamina's escape. "But I came in time to thwart them," he says. "You know me and my vigilance."

"You deserve a reward," says Sarastro ironically, and he orders that Monostatos be soundly whipped.

Slaves lead the protesting Moor away.

Sarastro gives orders for the two strangers to be admitted to the temple, but first, he says, they must be purified.

The priests lead Tamino and Papageno away. Sarastro takes Pamina's hand and they go into the temple together.

The opening scene of Act II is a grove of palm trees. Priests enter in a solemn procession. Sarastro enters with them. He tells the assembly that Tamino is waiting to join their religious order. He assures the group that the young man is kind and good and able to keep silent. The gods have chosen Pamina for this noble prince.

"Therefore," says Sarastro, "I have taken her from her mother. The proud queen seeks through superstition to destroy our temple, but she shall not succeed. Tamino shall become one of us and help us strengthen the power of goodness and wisdom."

However, there are ordeals awaiting Tamino before he can become a member of the order.

The scene changes to the court of the temple. Tamino and Papageno are led in by two priests.

The prince is ready to undergo the trials, but Papageno hesitates. One of the priests tells him that Sarastro has chosen a bride for him—a beautiful girl named Papagena. Papageno may see her, but first he must undergo the ordeals.

Papageno agrees that for the sight of his Papagena he will face any trial.

"You may see her, but you may not speak to her," the priest warns him. "Will you be strong enough to hold your tongue?"

"Oh, yes!" says Papageno.

The same warning applies to Tamino. He may see Pamina, but he must keep silent until Sarastro gives him permission to speak.

The priests leave, and the three ladies appear. They try to persuade Tamino and Papageno to flee from the enemies of the queen.

The bird-catcher wavers, but Tamino stands firm.

Threatening voices call from within the temple, and the ladies run out in confusion.

Priests enter and praise Tamino for his steadfastness. They lead him and Papageno away for another ordeal.

The next scene is a garden where Pamina lies asleep. Monostatos is there, gazing on her with longing.

The Queen of the Night appears.

"Go!" she orders Monostatos.

Pamina wakes. "Mother!" she cries, and Monostatos creeps away.

The queen gives her daughter a dagger. "It is for Sarastro," she says. "You will kill him."

She will not listen to Pamina's protests. "If he does not die by your hand," she tells the girl, "I renounce you forever!"

She disappears.

Pamina gazes fearfully at the dagger in her hand. She cannot bring herself to commit murder, yet she has never disobeyed her mother.

Monostatos has been hiding in the garden. Now he draws near. "Trust me," he says, and he takes the dagger from her. "There is only one way for you to save your mother and yourself."

"What is that?" asks Pamina.

"You must love me," he says.

"No!" cries Pamina.

"Then die!" he shouts, and he raises the dagger.

Unexpectedly Sarastro is there, holding the slave back. Monostatos kneels, protesting that he is innocent.

Sarastro orders him off, and Monostatos slinks away.

Pamina begs Sarastro not to punish her mother.

He reassures her. In this holy realm revenge is unknown and all men forgive their enemies.

The first scene of Act III is a hallway. Tamino and Papageno enter, led by the two priests. Tamino's flute and Papageno's bells have been taken away. The priests leave, after they have again cautioned the men to be silent.

Papageno begins to grumble. He would rather be back in his hut in the woods. These people, he complains, don't give him even a drop of water.

An old woman comes to him with a cup in her hands.

"Is that for me?" he asks.

"Yes, my angel," she answers.

There is water in the cup. Papageno drinks, and he and the woman sit down side by side. He asks how old she is.

"Eighteen years and two minutes," she answers.

Papageno thinks she must mean *eighty* years and two minutes. "Have you a sweetheart?" he asks.

"Of course," she says. "His name is Papageno."

He is startled. "Who are you?" he asks.

Before she can answer, there is a clap of thunder, and she goes hobbling off.

The three spirits appear, bringing back the magic flute and bells. A table rises out of the ground. Papageno is delighted to find it spread with food and drink.

Tamino plays the flute. The sound brings Pamina. She speaks to him joyfully, but he cannot answer. He has not yet been given permission to speak.

She appeals to Papageno. He is eating and drinking, and his mouth is so full that he can only mumble.

Again she speaks to Tamino. Does he no longer love her? Can he not see how she weeps for him?

Still he does not speak. Brokenhearted, she goes away.

A trumpet sounds, summoning Tamino and Papageno. Tamino drags the bird-catcher away from the table.

"Don't be in such a hurry," says Papageno. "We'll be there in plenty of time to be roasted."

The scene changes to a crypt inside a pyramid. The priests and Sarastro join in a chant praising Tamino for his obedience and courage.

The prince and Pamina are brought in. Two dangerous trials are still ahead for the prince.

Sarastro tells the girl, "Tamino waits to bid you farewell."

But when she starts toward the prince, he motions her away.

"If you love me as I love you," she says, "you would not be cold and silent."

Sarastro tells them both to have courage. He leads

the prince out of the crypt, while Pamina is led away
by the two priests.

The crypt grows dark. Papageno enters, feeling his
way and calling out for Tamino. Each time he reaches
a doorway, thunder crashes and flames bar his way.

He begins to weep.

A priest enters and tells him sternly that he deserves
to wander in darkness forever. However, the gods have
granted him pardon, although he will never know the
heavenly pleasure of the chosen ones.

Papageno replies that he doesn't care a fig about being
a chosen one. His greatest wish at the moment is for
a glass of wine.

The priest disappears. A great cup of wine rises out
of the earth. Papageno seizes it and drinks thirstily.

The wine brings a glow to his heart. Again he finds
himself longing for a sweetheart, and he plays the magic
bells to see what fortune they may bring to him.

The little old woman hobbles in.

"Here I am, my angel," she says, and she tells him
she is ready to become his little wife.

She advises him not to hesitate. "Give me your hand,
or you will be a prisoner here forever and live on bread
and water, shut off from the world, with no friends or
sweetheart."

Papageno decides that, after all, an old wife is better
than none. Giving her his hand, he tells her he will be

true, and he adds to himself, "Until I meet someone prettier."

"Do you swear it?" she asks.

"Yes, I swear it," he says.

At once she is transformed into a beautiful girl in a costume of feathers like that of the bird-catcher.

"Pa-Pa-Papagena!" stammers Papageno in delighted amazement. As he starts to embrace her, a priest enters.

"He is not yet worthy," says the priest, and he drags Papagena away.

In the next scene Pamina enters a garden of palm trees. She is in despair over what she thinks is Tamino's indifference, and she is ready to end her life. She carries a dagger. As she lifts it, the three spirits descend upon her and wrest it from her hand.

They tell her the prince is faithful, and they offer to lead her to him.

The next scene takes place among rocky caves. At the left is a fire, at the right is a waterfall. Two men in armor stand guard at a door in the rocks.

Tamino is led in by the two priests. The prince declares he is ready for the final test. In the distance Pamina calls to him. She has come to be with him through the last ordeal.

Tamino asks if he may break his silence. The priests grant him permission, and the two lovers greet each other rapturously.

Playing the magic flute, Tamino walks into the cave of fire, with Pamina beside him. They come out unharmed. Next they enter the cave of water. From this ordeal, too, they come safely.

Now the door of the temple is before them, lighted and open. Sarastro takes them inside.

In the next scene Papageno comes wandering into a garden. He believes Papagena is lost to him forever, and he has decided to hang himself.

He stops under a tree. This, he says, will be his gallows. He makes a noose ready and looks about him, hoping someone will stop him. If no one stops him before he counts three, he tells himself, the deed will be done.

He counts—one . . . two . . . two and a half . . . No one comes to his aid.

As he bids the world farewell, the three spirits arrive. They advise him to call to his love with the magic bells.

This had not occurred to Papageno. He takes out the bells and begins to play.

Magically Papagena appears. It is a moment of ecstasy for them both. They circle each other in a birdlike dance, and they plan a future in which many little Papagenos and Papagenas will come to bless their home.

The final scene is a rocky landscape. It is night. Monostatos enters with the Queen of the Night and the three ladies. He has been employed by the queen to kidnap

Pamina from the temple. In payment, the queen has promised him her daughter's hand. She is resolved to destroy Sarastro and all his followers.

But Sarastro's might falls on them in the form of a terrible storm. Monostatos, the queen, and the three ladies sink out of sight into the earth.

Brightness floods the landscape and the temple. Sarastro, Tamino, and Pamina stand before the temple door.

"The glory of the sun has conquered the night," says Sarastro. His followers gather. Together they praise the gods and bless the triumph of courage, wisdom, and goodness.

60-9611

# The Barber of Seville

The original *Barber of Seville* was a play by the French dramatist Beaumarchais. It was first performed in 1775. Soon afterward the Italian composer, Paisiello, composed an opera based on the story. His works are seldom heard today, but in his lifetime he was greatly admired.

In 1816 another *Barber of Seville* appeared. The new opera was by a young Italian, Gioacchino Rossini. He was much criticized for daring to choose a subject already set to music by Paisiello.

When the opera was first performed—in Rome, on February 20, 1816—the audience drowned out the music with hisses and catcalls. But on the second night it was given a hearing. By the end of the third performance it was a success.

The opening scene is a square in Seville, in front of

Doctor Bartolo's house. It is morning, not yet daylight. Count Almaviva appears with his servant, Fiorello, and a band of musicians. The count has come to serenade Rosina, ward of Doctor Bartolo. He has seen her and fallen in love with her, although they have never met. The old doctor keeps her under lock and key because he hopes to marry her himself.

Almaviva sings his serenade and sends his servant and the musicians away. While he waits for Rosina to come to the window, he hears someone coming toward the square. Not wishing to be recognized, he hides under the portico of the house.

Figaro enters. He is playing a guitar and singing a song about himself and his great importance. He is a barber by trade, but he also serves as a doctor, a carrier of letters, and even as an adviser to people in love.

He spies Almaviva. The two recognize each other.

"What are you doing in Seville?" asks Figaro.

Almaviva answers that he hopes to win Rosina.

Figaro offers to help him. "In this house," he says, "I am the barber, hairdresser, surgeon, chemist, druggist, and confidential agent!"

The window opens. The men are not sure who may be watching, and they hide under the portico.

Rosina comes out onto the balcony. She has a letter for her unknown admirer and is disappointed because he is nowhere in sight.

Her guardian, Doctor Bartolo, comes out behind her and suspiciously asks to see the paper in her hand.

"It is only the words of a song," she says, and she lets the paper fall. Almaviva picks it up.

Bartolo suspects he is being tricked. He orders Rosina into the house.

Almaviva reads the letter. "My guardian is going to leave the house," Rosina has written. "As soon as he is gone, find some way of letting me know your name and your intentions."

Bartolo leaves the house. Almaviva and Figaro overhear him say to a servant, "While I am gone, let no one in except Don Basilio." He goes away, muttering that he must arrange to marry Rosina as quickly as possible.

Almaviva asks who Don Basilio is.

"A matchmaker, a scoundrel, and a hypocrite," answers Figaro. "Just now he is Rosina's music teacher."

Almaviva considers what he will say to Rosina when they meet. He decides not to tell her at first that he is a count. "Then," he says, "I'll be sure she loves me and not my wealth or title."

Figaro sees Rosina back at the window. He hands the count his guitar and urges him to sing to her.

The count serenades Rosina, telling her in song that his name is Lindoro and he adores her.

She is being watched from inside the house. She has to leave quickly.

"I must see her again!" says Almaviva.

Figaro has a plan. He will disguise the count as a soldier. Then the count can pretend he has been quartered in the house of the doctor.

The next scene is a room in Doctor Bartolo's house. Rosina is there alone, thinking of Lindoro. She has already determined that he shall be hers. "I am soft, I am gentle," she says, "but everyone must learn that I will have my way."

She has written another letter to Lindoro. She hopes Figaro will deliver it.

The barber enters. Before he and Rosina can exchange more than a few words, they hear the doctor's footsteps. Figaro hides, but the doctor knows he is in the house.

"Have you seen that quack of a barber?" he asks.

She answers, "I have, and I find him pleasant and entertaining," and she goes out.

Bartolo wonders what they have been talking about. He tries to find out from two servants, Berta and Ambrogio, but Ambrogio can only yawn and Berta has fits of sneezing. At last he drives them out of his sight.

Basilio, the music master, arrives. He has news for the doctor. Count Almaviva has been seen in the neighborhood, and he may well be the unknown man who has been pursuing Rosina.

Basilio suggests they spread slander about the count so that he will have to leave the city.

Bartolo thinks his own plan is better—that he marry his ward at once. "When she is my wife," he says, "I'll put an end to her flirtations."

He and Basilio leave to draw up the marriage contract. Figaro comes out of hiding. Rosina returns, and he tells her what he has overheard—that her guardian has decided to marry her at once.

"Nonsense!" she says, and she asks the barber about the young man with whom he was talking under her window that morning.

"He is a promising young man," says Figaro. "Poor, but good-hearted, and madly in love with a girl named Rosina." This young Lindoro will soon be here, he says. All she need do is write a letter saying she expects him.

She answers that she could not possibly do such a thing. Then she gives him the letter she has already written.

Figaro takes the letter away. The doctor comes back and again tries to find out what she and the barber were talking about.

"He spoke of trifles," she says.

"Did he bring an answer to the letter you dropped from the window this morning?" he asks.

"What letter?" she asks.

If she wrote no letter, he asks, why are there inkstains on her finger?

She scorched her finger, she tells him, and she heard that ink is good for burns.

"Six sheets of paper were on the desk this morning," he says. "Now one is missing."

She answers that she wrapped some sweets in it.

"The pen has just been used," he says.

"I used it to draw a flower on my embroidery," she answers.

He warns her not to drive him too far with her deceit. In the future, he says, he will lock the doors and windows so that even a fly cannot get in.

Count Almaviva comes noisily into the house, disguised as a soldier. He has been quartered here, he tells the indignant doctor. While Bartolo's back is turned, the count lets Rosina know that he is Lindoro.

The doctor searches in his desk. He finds what he is looking for—an official paper showing that he is not obliged to keep soldiers in his home.

The count refuses to go. "Drop your handkerchief," he whispers to Rosina. She drops it, and he returns it along with a letter.

Bartolo sees the letter and demands it.

It is only the laundry list, she tells him. Bartolo tears the paper from her hand, to find that it *is* the laundry list, which Rosina has hastily substituted for the letter.

All is confusion. Basilio and the servant, Berta, have entered and are adding their voices to the din.

Figaro comes in and asks what is the matter. He has heard the noise all the way out in the street.

An officer of the guard and several soldiers come to enforce law and order. Doctor Bartolo points to the disguised count and shouts, "That beast has threatened me!"

The count takes the officer aside and explains that he is really a nobleman. The officer is all politeness, and he promptly withdraws his soldiers.

The uproar continues, with everyone talking at once, and the curtain falls.

Act II takes place that afternoon in Doctor Bartolo's library. The doctor is puzzling over the affair of the soldier. He suspects Count Almaviva behind it all.

Again the count appears. He has taken a new disguise —that of a music master. He introduces himself as Don Alonso, professor of music and Basilio's pupil. Basilio is ill, he says.

Doctor Bartolo is suspicious. The count realizes that if he is to see Rosina again he must quickly win the doctor's confidence.

He has news of Count Almaviva, he says. This morning he happened to be in the lodgings the count had just left. There he found a letter written by Rosina. If Rosina could see the letter that was so carelessly left behind, it might persuade her that her lover is not true to her.

Doctor Bartolo examines the letter the count hands him. It is indeed Rosina's handwriting.

The count suggests if he could see the lady he might find a way to blacken Almaviva's character.

"Bravo!" says the doctor. "I can see you are truly a pupil of Basilio."

He brings Rosina into the library and introduces the new music master. She soon recognizes him as her lover, Lindoro.

He sits beside her at the piano and pretends to give her a singing lesson. The doctor sits close by.

Figaro brings in his barber's basin and announces that this is Bartolo's day to be shaved.

The doctor hands him a bunch of keys. "Go to my room," he says, "and fetch the soap and towel."

Figaro goes out. There is a crash of breaking dishes.

"I was a fool to send him!" cries Bartolo, and he rushes out.

The lovers have a few minutes alone together.

By the time Bartolo and the barber return, Figaro has stolen the key to the balcony.

As the doctor settles himself to be shaved, Basilio appears. The conspirators gaze at him in consternation.

Doctor Bartolo inquires about Basilio's illness.

Figaro and the count give him no chance to answer. They insist he actually *is* ill—much too ill to be out.

"You have scarlet fever," says Figaro.

"You need strong medicine," says the count, and he secretly presses a purse into Basilio's hand.

Basilio is bewildered, but when the others join in bidding him farewell, he takes the money and leaves.

Figaro prepares to shave Doctor Bartolo.

Rosina and the count pretend to be studying music. With their heads close together, they plan to elope at midnight. It will be easy, says the count, because Figaro has given him the key to the balcony.

The doctor overhears part of the plans. "Scoundrels! Robbers!" he shouts, and he drives the three conspirators out of the room.

He summons the servants and sends Ambrogio to fetch Basilio. He tells Berta to guard the door. Then, deciding she is not to be trusted, he goes to guard it himself. Berta leaves, after complaining that this household is surely going mad.

The doctor returns with Basilio. They are discussing the music master who calls himself Don Alonso.

"I believe he was sent here by the count," says Bartolo.

"I tell you, he was the count himself," says Basilio.

Bartolo declares he must wait no longer. The contract must be drawn up for his marriage to Rosina.

Basilio doubts that the lawyer will come out to draw up the contract tonight because of the pouring rain. Besides, the lawyer has business with Figaro. A contract is being drawn up for the marriage of the barber's niece.

Bartolo suspects he is being tricked again. "Bring the lawyer here this instant!" he says. He gives Basilio the key to the front door and hurries him off.

The doctor has a new idea. He takes a letter from his pocket—Rosina's letter given him by the supposed Don Alonso. He calls Rosina. "I'm sorry to break the news to you," he tells her, "but you have given your affection to one who only laughs at you. This will prove it."

He shows her the letter. He convinces her that her lover has turned it over to Count Almaviva. "He and the barber have resolved to place you in the count's power," he says.

Count Almaviva's name is strange to Rosina. She knows him only as Lindoro. She is in despair, then she grows angry.

In her indignation, she agrees to marry Bartolo, and she tells him of the plans she and her lover have made. "At midnight," she says, "he and Figaro will come to take me away."

Then, says Doctor Bartolo, he will have them arrested as robbers.

He and Rosina leave.

The storm rises and dies. Figaro and the count put up a ladder and climb in through the window.

Rosina enters. She sees the count and denounces him.

It is time for him to end the deception. Lindoro and Almaviva are one and the same, he tells her.

The rapture of their love is cut short by Figaro. He tells them he has just seen two persons under the window, and the ladder has been taken away.

They hide in one side of the room.

Two men enter. Figaro recognizes one as Basilio.

"Who is the other?" asks the count.

"It's my friend, the lawyer," says Figaro. "That is good!" He steps boldly forward and speaks to the lawyer. "Do you remember that tonight I hired you to draw up a marriage contract between Count Almaviva and my niece?" he asks. "By accident the parties have met here. Have you the contract with you?"

The lawyer has brought it. The count bribes Basilio to keep quiet and serve as a witness.

Figaro introduces Rosina as his niece. The lawyer marries her to the count.

As Almaviva kisses the hand of his bride, Doctor Bartolo comes in with an officer and a patrol of soldiers. "There are the robbers!" says the doctor, pointing to Figaro and the count.

The count reveals his identity. He is the Count Almaviva, and Rosina is now the countess.

Doctor Bartolo has to accept the situation. Not only has he lost Rosina, but he is expected to pay the bride's dowry money to the count. Almaviva tells him to keep the dowry. The doctor is grateful for this crumb of comfort. By the time the curtain falls, even he is smiling.

# Lucia di Lammermoor

The Italian composer Gaetano Donizetti was at the height of his fame when he composed *Lucia di Lammermoor*. The story is based on Sir Walter Scott's novel, *The Bride of Lammermoor*. On September 26, 1835, the opera had its triumphant world premiere in Naples.

The setting of *Lucia* is sixteenth-century Scotland. Act I begins near Ravenswood Castle in the hills of Lammermoor. Castle guards are searching for a mysterious prowler who has been seen on the grounds.

While the other men continue the search, Normanno, captain of the guards, stays behind to speak with Enrico Ashton and Raimondo Bidebent. Ashton is lord of Ravenswood. Bidebent is a tutor and family friend.

Lord Ashton is lamenting his ill fortune. His family will be ruined, he declares, unless he can arrange a wealthy marriage for his sister, Lucia.

"She still mourns the death of her mother," says Bidebent. "How can she think of love and marriage?"

Lucia is no stranger to thoughts of love, says Normanno. He tells of the man who one day saved her from a maddened bull. She fell in love with her rescuer, and since then she has seen him often.

Lord Ashton demands the name of the man.

Normanno is not certain, but he suspects the man is Edgardo, who is Ashton's neighbor and has long been his enemy. Once Ravenswood belonged to Edgardo's family. Lord Ashton killed Edgardo's father and took possession of the estate.

The guards return. They have seen the prowler at close range. Although he escaped, they were able to recognize him. The man was Edgardo.

Beside himself with rage, Lord Ashton swears vengeance on his hated enemy.

The scene changes to the castle garden. Lucia enters with her companion, Alisa.

Lucia has come to meet Edgardo. While she waits, she keeps glancing fearfully at the old fountain. She recalls that in this garden long ago a Ravenswood killed the lady who loved him. Now her spirit is said to haunt the fountain.

"Once," says Lucia, with a shudder, "I saw the shadowy face of the lady as she stood at the edge of the fountain."

Alisa believes this is surely a warning. She begs Lucia to give up these dangerous meetings with Edgardo, but the girl refuses to listen.

Footsteps approach. Alisa goes back into the castle, and Edgardo comes into the garden.

He tells Lucia he must bid her good-by for a while. He is being sent to France on a political mission. He has an idea of trying to make peace with Lord Ashton before he leaves, so that her brother might consent to their marriage.

It would be useless, she answers.

"Why must he go on persecuting me!" bursts out Edgardo. "Is it not enough that he killed my father and robbed me of my inheritance? Will he be satisfied with nothing but my death?"

Once Edgardo, too, vowed vengeance. Then he met Lucia, and his heart was softened. Now he hopes somehow to end this bitter feud.

He and Lucia exchange rings in token of their love, and they bid each other a tender farewell.

Act II takes place in Ravenswood Castle. Several months have passed. Ashton is telling Normanno that a marriage has been arranged for Lucia. Unless she proves stubborn, she will marry the wealthy Lord Arturo Bucklaw today.

Normanno does not think she will resist. Edgardo's messages from France have not been allowed to reach her, and the rumor has been spread that he has taken a bride.

"She is coming," says Ashton, and he asks quickly for the letter he has had written. Normanno gives it to him. It is a forged letter prepared as proof that Edgardo has been unfaithful to Lucia.

Normanno leaves to escort Arturo Bucklaw to the castle.

Lucia enters. She is languid and pale.

Ashton insists that she marry Lord Bucklaw. "Always before you have obeyed me," he says. "Will you disobey me now?"

She answers that she is promised to someone else.

"You have given your promise to a traitor," he says, and he hands her the forged letter. Reading it, she begins to weep.

From another part of the castle comes festive music. "It is your wedding music," Ashton tells her.

She begs him not to force this marriage upon her. He threatens to punish both her and Edgardo if she remains stubborn. Angrily he leaves her.

Bidebent comes to Lucia. He believes Edgardo is faithless. He advises her to accept the marriage her brother has arranged, and she yields at last.

The scene changes to a hall in the castle. Wedding guests have arrived, and Lord Arturo Bucklaw enters. The wedding party waits for Lucia.

Lord Ashton tells the bridegroom, "Pay no attention if she seems sad. She still grieves for her mother."

Alisa and Bidebent lead Lucia into the hall. The girl moves in a daze. She allows herself to be led to the table where the marriage contract is to be signed.

Arturo signs the paper. Lucia hesitates. Her brother commands her fiercely, "Sign it!" and she obeys.

As she leans on Bidebent's arm, a black-cloaked figure bursts into the hall. It is Edgardo.

In a terrible voice he denounces Lucia and her brother. Lord Ashton is alarmed in spite of himself. Lucia prays for strength and courage, while Alisa, the bridegroom, and Bidebent offer her consolation.

Ashton and Arturo draw their swords, and Edgardo prepares to defend himself. In a tone of authority Bidebent orders them to put away their weapons. They obey.

Lord Ashton asks Edgardo why he has dared to come here.

Edgardo answers that Lucia is promised to him.

Bidebent shows him the marriage contract. Pointing to Lucia's signature, Edgardo asks her, "Is this your writing—tell me!"

She answers faintly, "Yes!"

He gives back her ring. He snatches his ring from her, throws it down, and stamps on it.

"At last I know you!" he cries.

The men of the party move toward him. He throws

away his sword and offers his breast for them to strike. Now that all he held dear is lost to him, he will gladly die, he says.

Lucia pleads that his life be spared. Arturo and the wedding guests order him out of the castle. Alisa begs him to go. Lord Ashton repeats his vow of vengeance, as Bidebent lifts his voice in an appeal to reason.

Act III begins that night in Wolfscrag Tower, where Edgardo lives alone. Lord Ashton enters. He challenges Edgardo to a duel.

They agree to meet at dawn near the graveyards of Ravenswood.

The scene shifts to the castle, where guests are still celebrating the wedding. Bidebent comes into the hall. In a hushed and trembling voice he tells them that Lucia has slain her husband.

She appears before the horrified guests. She is pale and vacant-eyed. In her madness she sees again the specter of the fountain. Then, radiantly happy, she fancies that she and Edgardo have come to the church to be married.

Lord Ashton enters. Is it true, he asks, that his sister has committed this terrible crime?

It is all too true, answers Bidebent, but because of her madness she is not to blame. He says accusingly, "It is you who have brought her to this."

Lucia raves on in delirium until she falls into Alisa's

arms. Alisa leads her away. Bowed down with grief and remorse, Lord Ashton follows.

Bidebent looks at Normanno, who cowers before him. "Vile informer!" he says, "it was through you that all was known," and he orders the captain from the castle.

The final scene is in the Ravenswood graveyard. Edgardo is wandering in the darkness among the tombs of his ancestors. He sees the castle blazing with lights. All is happiness there, he tells himself, while he is ready to die of despair.

Mourners come from the castle. Edgardo asks them why they are weeping.

They tell him of Arturo's death and Lucia's madness, and now Lucia, too, is dead. "With her last breath, she called for you," they say.

Edgardo begins to understand that he has wronged her. He starts toward the castle. Bidebent, who has come with the mourners, holds him back, reminding him that Lucia is dead.

Edgardo sees nothing left in life. He draws a dagger and stabs himself. Hoping to meet his beloved in heaven, he dies, the last of the Ravenswoods, among the tombs of his ancestors.

# Tannhauser

Sometime between 1839 and 1842 Richard Wagner first considered *Tannhauser* as the subject for an opera. He was living in Paris at the time, and he had found the story among German legends of the Middle Ages.

In 1843, at his home in Dresden, Germany, he finished the libretto. The following year he finished the musical score. *Tannhauser* had its world premiere at the Dresden opera house on October 19, 1845, with the composer conducting.

The opening scene shows the Venusberg, dwelling place of Venus, the goddess of love. At the side is a cave. In the background is a lake. Sirens, nymphs, and other inhabitants of Venus' court move about in the rose-colored dimness.

Venus is reclining on a couch. Tannhauser, a minstrel knight, kneels before her. He lifts his head and looks

71

about him, as if waking from sleep. He has dreamed of chiming bells, he tells her, an earthly sound long strange to him.

He wonders how long he has been here, lost in Venus' enchantment.

She fears he is growing weary of her. "Have you forgotten how your heart was in mourning until I consoled you?" she asks, and she commands him to sing in praise of love.

Obediently he takes up his harp and sings her praises, but he adds that only a god can live in perfect bliss. A mortal such as himself must know pain as well as pleasure. He asks her to set him free.

She refuses, but he continues to ask, until she tells him angrily that she will hold him here no longer. She predicts that he will come back to her, humbled and sad.

She vanishes. Tannhauser finds himself suddenly on earth in the valley below the Venusberg. To the right is a shrine to the Virgin Mary. Nearby sits a shepherd boy playing his pipe. Sheep bells are ringing in the meadow beyond.

A pilgrim band comes into the valley. The shepherd calls, "Godspeed to Rome!"

Tannhauser kneels as the procession crosses the valley. Deeply moved, he prays to God and vows he will not rest until he has been pardoned for his sins.

The landgrave, count of Thuringia, and a party of

minstrel knights come down the hill. They greet Tannhauser as their lost one.

Wolfram, the minstrel who was once his dearest friend,
welcomes him warmly. The others are more reserved.
They remember that Tannhauser left them in haughti-
ness and pride. The landgrave asks him where he has
stayed so long.

"In strange and distant places," answers Tannhauser.
"We meet as friends, now let me go in peace."

They ask him to stay. He answers that he is doomed to
wander on alone.

Wolfram speaks a name—"Elisabeth."

Tannhauser stands entranced. "Elisabeth!" he repeats.

Wolfram turns to the landgrave and says, "Let me tell
him of the prize he has won."

The landgrave grants permission.

Wolfram reminds Tannhauser of the days of the minstrels' song contests. Tannhauser's songs won the heart
of Elisabeth, the landgrave's daughter, but after he went
away she withdrew from the world and came no more to
the contests of song.

Wolfram begs him to return to her.

The other minstrels and the landgrave add their pleas
to his, until Tannhauser yields.

The second act begins in the Hall of Song, where the
contests are held. Elisabeth enters, radiantly happy now
that Tannhauser has returned.

Wolfram and Tannhauser come to the doorway, and Tannhauser goes forward alone to meet Elisabeth. Their reunion is a joyous one. She confesses that while he was away, all happiness was gone from her life.

After Tannhauser has left the hall, the landgrave enters. Knights and nobles are assembling for a contest of song, he tells his daughter. All will be here, since they know she will be in the hall again to award the victory wreath.

From the balcony Elisabeth and her father watch the guests arrive. The minstrels assemble. The landgrave announces the theme of the contest: "What is love, and by what signs shall we know it?"

The minstrel whose song is judged best shall receive the prize from Elisabeth.

Wolfram is the first contestant. He sings of pure, unselfish love.

Tannhauser has been sitting quietly, as if in a dream. For the moment he has forgotten Elisabeth and the Hall of Song. Once more in the spell of the Venusberg, he springs to his feet and bursts into a song praising Venus and the unholy love he has known.

Elisabeth is dismayed. The other ladies leave the hall. The landgrave and the other men turn on Tannhauser. Crying out that this insult must be avenged, they draw their swords.

Elisabeth throws herself protectingly in front of Tannhauser. "What right have you to judge this man?" she says. "As Christians, you should show mercy."

The men put away their swords. Already Tannhauser is stricken with shame.

The landgrave tells him solemnly, "One path alone can save you." Another band of pilgrims is gathering nearby for the journey to the sacred city of Rome. He must join them and seek forgiveness for his sins.

The scene of Act III is the valley below Wartburg Hill. It is sunset. Elisabeth is kneeling before the shrine to the Virgin. Wolfram comes near and pauses. He gazes on her with love, although he knows his love is a hopeless one.

The time is near for Tannhauser's return. Every day Elisabeth has prayed to the Virgin that he may be forgiven.

Pilgrims enter. Elisabeth watches them, seeking Tannhauser. He is not among them. Now she believes he will never come back to her.

After the pilgrims have gone, she kneels again before the shrine. She prays that she may be freed from the earth and enter into God's kingdom.

As she rises, she sees Wolfram. He comes toward her, and she motions him back.

He asks if they may walk together.

Silently she shakes her head, and she goes alone up the path to Wartburg Hill.

Wolfram watches night fall over the valley—like death's dark shadow, he thinks. But he finds comfort in the light of the evening star.

A ragged pilgrim comes slowly along the path. He is leaning heavily on a staff.

It is Tannhauser.

"What brings you here?" asks Wolfram anxiously, for unless Tannhauser's sins have been forgiven, he has no right to return.

Tannhauser answers in a strange, wild voice that he is searching for the path back to the Venusberg. He has been to Rome. For Elisabeth's sake he tried to make his peace with God.

"I saw him who holds the keys to heaven," he says. "Thousands he forgave that day, but when I confessed my sins, he said, 'If you have dwelled in the Venusberg, you are accursed, and as the dead staff I hold will never put forth a leaf, so shall you never know salvation.' "

He calls to Venus.

Clouds gather over the valley. A rose-colored glow lights the sky. Through the mist appears the goddess, lying on her couch.

She welcomes him to the Venusberg.

Wolfram tries to hold him back, and Tannhauser tears himself away. Wolfram speaks Elisabeth's name.

Tannhauser pauses. From the distance voices rise in a chant for the dead. Torches gleam through the mist.

Men come in sight carrying a bier on which is the body of Elisabeth.

With a despairing cry, Venus fades from sight.

Tannhauser goes to the bier.

"Holy Elisabeth, pray for me," he whispers. Dying, he sinks to the ground.

Pilgrims enter. One of them holds high a staff covered with green leaves. It is the symbol that Tannhauser's soul has been redeemed.

# Lohengrin

For the story of *Lohengrin,* Wagner turned again to German legend. He sketched the libretto in 1845 and finished the score two years later.

In 1849 he fled from Germany to avoid arrest for his part in the uprising against the government. From Paris he sent a copy of *Lohengrin* to the pianist-composer, Franz Liszt, in Weimar, Germany. Through the influence of Liszt the new opera was produced. Its first performance was in Weimar on August 28, 1850.

Years later Wagner, still in exile, complained that he was the only German who had not heard *Lohengrin.* Not until 1861 was he able to hear it, in Vienna.

The setting of the opera is Brabant, in what is now Belgium, during the tenth century. The first scene is a plain near the River Scheldt, with the city of Antwerp in the background.

Telramund, count of Brabant, and Ortrud, his wife, have come for a meeting with their royal visitor, King Henry of Germany. The king seeks help against enemies who have placed his country in danger.

The count can promise no help because of the inner strife in Brabant. The former ruler has died, leaving a son, Gottfried, and a daughter, Elsa. Gottfried has disappeared. Telramund has accused Elsa of having caused his death, and at the same time he has declared himself ruler of Brabant.

King Henry sends for Elsa so that she may be judged.

Timidly the girl appears before him. She tells of a dream she has had, in which heaven sent a knight to defend her.

The king is impressed by her look of innocence. He tells the count, "It will be ill for you if you accuse her wrongly."

Telramund insists that she is guilty. "Here I stand. Here is my sword!" he cries. "Which of you dares to fight against my honor?"

The king consents to a trial by combat. He asks Elsa to name the knight who will defend her.

She does not know his name. She only knows that heaven will send the knight she has seen in her dream. Then she will give him all her possessions and, if he wishes it, he shall have her hand in marriage.

Trumpets are sounded. A herald calls, "He who comes here to fight for Elsa of Brabant, step forth at once!"

There is no answer.

Telramund says in triumph, "This proves my cause is right."

Again the trumpets are sounded. Again there is silence.

Telramund's attendants and the king's soldiers speak in low voices. "By this silence heaven dictates," they tell one another.

Elsa kneels in prayer.

On the river a boat appears, drawn by a swan. A man stands in the boat—a knight in silver armor with a golden horn at his side.

People draw near the river bank, gazing in awe. The knight steps ashore, tenderly bids the swan farewell, and sends it away. He offers himself as Elsa's champion.

"If I am victorious in the fight, will you be my wife?" he asks her.

"Yes," she answers. "Freely I give my life to you."

He asks her to make a promise. If he should become her husband, she must never ask his name or rank or from where he came.

She gives him her promise.

He and Telramund face each other in combat. They fight fiercely. The knight strikes Telramund down, but generously spares his life.

The swan-knight's victory clears Elsa of the charge

against her. The king leads her to the arms of her champion. It is a moment of great rejoicing for all except the defeated Telramund and his wife.

The scene of Act II is the fortress of Antwerp. In the background are the Pallas, where the knights have their quarters, and the Kemenate, quarters of the women. To the right is the doorway of the cathedral.

It is night, and the windows of the Pallas are brightly lighted. On the cathedral steps sit the two outcasts, Telramund and Ortrud.

He blames her for their downfall.

"Was it not you," he says, "who told me you saw Elsa drown her brother in a pool? Did you not then cause me to turn from Elsa and take you as my wife instead?"

Ortrud admits that this is true.

And because she led him from the path of honor, he says, heaven has turned against him.

It was not heaven that caused him to lose the fight, she answers; it was his own weakness and cowardice. She is not yet ready to admit defeat. The swan-knight must be overthrown. She knows something of witchcraft, and she believes the knight owes his strength to a magic spell. If they can learn the secret of his name and rank, the spell will be broken. It is through Elsa that the secret can be discovered.

"First we must fill her with mistrust," says Ortrud, "then charge him with sorcery and deceit."

Elsa comes out upon the balcony of the Kemenate.

Ortrud orders her husband out of sight and calls pathetically up to the girl, "How have I ever harmed you?"

Elsa is moved to pity. She leaves the balcony and comes down to admit Ortrud to the Kemenate.

She promises to take Ortrud to the swan-knight. "He will forgive you—and Telramund, too—as I forgive you," she says.

Ortrud bows in mock humility. "What gratitude can ever repay you!" she says. "I am a wretched being, far below you, but one small power is left to me. Perhaps I can use it to save you from sorrow."

"What do you mean?" asks the girl.

The swan-knight came here through some strange magic, says Ortrud. What if he should leave in the same way?

There is no room in Elsa's heart for doubt. She pities Ortrud for her lack of faith.

As they go into the Kemenate together, Telramund watches, certain that his honor is soon to be avenged.

It is now daylight. Nobles and townspeople gather before the cathedral, and Telramund again moves into hiding.

The royal herald comes from the Pallas and proclaims the king's decree—that Telramund shall be banished and Elsa's future husband shall rule Brabant.

Four nobles, friends of Telramund, begin to talk

among themselves. "Why should a stranger take our country from us?" asks one.

"But who will dare oppose him?" asks another.

Telramund has overheard. He speaks to them: "Soon I shall declare the knight an imposter." He and the noblemen leave together.

Ladies come from the Kemenate, conducting Elsa,

who is in her bridal dress. Near the end of the procession is Ortrud. She is scornful and proudly aloof.

As Elsa reaches the cathedral, Ortrud runs up the steps, stands before her, and forces her back.

"Although I bow before you, I am not your slave!" she cries. "Now I seek vengeance!"

In a passionate outburst, she defends her husband. Before he was overthrown, all the nation knew him as a man of honor. But what of Elsa's bridegroom? "A stranger here," says Ortrud, "whose very name you do not know."

"He is true and noble," answers Elsa.

He may seem so, says Ortrud, but who knows his race or if he is of noble birth?

The king and the swan-knight come out of the Pallas and press through the crowd. The knight takes Elsa in his arms. Sternly he orders Ortrud to leave.

The procession continues, but again it is halted, this time by Telramund.

He was defeated only by black magic, he declares, and he accuses the swan-knight of sorcery. If the knight has nothing to hide, he says, let him tell his name and rank and place of birth.

The knight replies that there is no need for him to answer. He has already proved his worth.

The king accepts his word, but Elsa trembles. In spite of herself, she has begun to doubt.

Telramund speaks to her secretly. She can learn the truth, he tells her. If the knight is wounded, ever so slightly, he will be bound to reveal all his secrets to her.

"At night I shall be near," says Telramund. "Call me."

The swan-knight discovers him there and drives him away. The procession moves on into the cathedral.

The first scene of Act III is the bridal chamber, where the wedding party leads the bride and groom.

When Elsa and the swan-knight are alone, he tenderly speaks her name.

"How sweet my name sounds when you speak it!" she says, "yet I may never hear the sound of yours." Now that they are married, she says, surely she may hope to know his name.

He reminds her of her promise.

"But if you never tell me," she says, "how can I trust you?"

She asks the forbidden questions.

He cries in anguish, "What have you done!"

Telramund appears with his friends, the four noblemen. They rush at the knight with drawn swords.

He springs to defend himself. He strikes a single blow with his sword, and Telramund falls lifeless. The four noblemen kneel fearfully before the knight.

Elsa has fallen in a faint. The knight places her on the couch.

"Despair!" he says. "Now all our happiness is fled."

Elsa, reviving, whispers, "Heaven, pity me!"

At a sign from the knight, the four nobles rise. He commands them to carry Telramund's body to the king. He calls Elsa's ladies and orders them to prepare her for a meeting with King Henry. In the presence of the king, he says, he will tell her what she wished to know.

The scene changes to the plain beside the river. The army of Brabant assembles, now ready to aid King Henry against his enemies. The king and his forces arrive.

As the men salute King Henry, the four nobles arrive, carrying the body of Telramund.

Elsa enters, escorted by her ladies. She moves slowly, with trembling steps.

The swan-knight, in his silver armor, greets the king. The soldiers call out, "We wait for you to lead us to victory."

The knight answers that he may not lead the armies. He has come here only to be judged. He tells how Telramund came upon him in the night and tried to take his life. "Say whether or not I was right to slay him."

The king answers that Telramund deserved to die.

The knight speaks again. "My wife was lured to break her vow," he says. "You heard her promise not to ask my name. The promise has been broken."

There is no longer any need to keep the secret. His home is a castle on Mount Monsalvat. In the castle is the Holy Grail, the cup from which Christ drank at the last supper. The sacred cup is guarded by men who are without sin. Heaven protects them and gives them power against evil, but once their secret is known, they can no longer live in the world of men.

"I was sent here, a Knight of the Holy Grail," he tells them. "My father is Parsifal. My name is Lohengrin." He speaks to Elsa, "Now I must leave you forever!"

The king begs the knight to stay. Lohengrin answers that this is forbidden.

The swan-boat is in sight on the river. Lohengrin greets the swan. He has a last word for Elsa. If he had stayed for a single year, he could have restored her lost brother, Gottfried. "If he comes, you will receive him alone," he says. "Give him this sword, this golden horn, and this ring. He will conquer when he raises the sword. The horn will help him in his hour of need. And when he looks on the ring he will think of the one who freed you from danger."

Ortrud steps from among the assembled people. Exultant in her triumph, she cries tauntingly that it was she who caused young Gottfried to disappear. She cast a spell upon him and changed him to a swan—the same swan that draws Lohengrin's boat. Now that the knight must leave before a year, Gottfried must remain a swan forever.

Lohengrin has heard her evil confession. He kneels and silently prays for a miracle.

A white dove flies low and hovers over the boat. The swan changes to a handsome young man—Elsa's brother, Gottfried.

Lohengrin hails him as the new ruler of Brabant. Then he steps into the boat, which the dove draws away.

Ortrud shrieks in terror as she recognizes Gottfried.

Elsa gazes after the swan-boat.

"My husband! My husband!" she cries. Falling back, she dies in Gottfried's arms, as Lohengrin slowly disappears.

# Tristan and Isolde

From 1849 to 1860 Richard Wagner was a political exile from his native Germany. During most of this time he lived in Switzerland. In 1857 he wrote the libretto based on the old Celtic legend of Tristan, and two years later he finished the musical score. The first performance of *Tristan and Isolde* was in Munich on June 10, 1865.

The opening scene is the deck of a ship at sea. Part of the deck is closed off by a curtain. In the enclosed space are the Irish princess, Isolde, and her maid, Brangaene. Isolde is lying on a couch. Brangaene is looking out to sea.

The song of a sailor arouses the princess. "Where are we?" she asks.

Brangaene answers that the ship is nearing Cornwall.

Isolde calls on the powers of magic to wreck the ship before it reaches land.

Anxious and alarmed, Brangaene asks Isolde what it is that troubles her.

Isolde does not answer. Instead she cries out for air. The maid opens the curtain, and the ship is revealed all the way to the stern. Sailors are busy about the mainmast. Beyond them are knights and their attendants. Apart from the others stands Tristan, a knight of Cornwall. His servant, Kurvenal, is with him.

Isolde gazes at Tristan. "So this is the hero who is ashamed to look at me!" she says in bitter scorn. "He hides from me while he brings me to be the bride of his king." She orders Brangaene, "Go and ask him to come to me if he dares."

The maid takes the message to Tristan.

He answers, "If I leave my place, how can I pilot the ship safely to King Mark?"

Kurvenal speaks up loudly so that Isolde can hear. It is hardly for the princess to give orders to Tristan, he says, since Cornwall is no longer ruled by Ireland. He sings mockingly of Morold, the Irish warrior who came to Cornwall to collect taxes and was slain by Tristan.

Brangaene returns to Isolde and closes the curtain.

Angered and humiliated, the princess says to her maid, "You know my shame. Now hear what caused it."

She tells of a wounded man who came to Ireland in a drifting boat. She healed him and tended him faithfully. Then she learned that he was none other than Tristan. Not only was he of an enemy country, but he had slain Morold, the Irish hero who was to have been her husband. Tristan had been wounded in his fight with Morold. Knowing her magic powers of healing, he had disguised himself and come to her to be made well.

"I stood above him with his own sword," she says, "ready to avenge Morold's death. But when he looked deep in my eyes, I could not strike."

He went away. She hoped he would never trouble her again. But he returned to Ireland to fetch her as an unwilling bride for his uncle, old King Mark of Cornwall.

Brangaene tries to console her. "Remember your mother's skill in magic," she says. "Do you think she would send you unprepared on this journey?"

This reminds Isolde of the casket her mother has given her. In it are magic potions for healing wounds and easing pain, and there are potions of love and death.

Brangaene brings the casket. Isolde takes a vial from it. "This will do me good!" she says.

It is the death potion.

Kurvenal enters and tells the women to be up and moving. The ship will soon land, and Isolde must be ready so that Tristan may escort her to King Mark.

Isolde tells him, "It is not right that I should walk beside Tristan until I have pardoned him for the wrong he has done me. And he may not have my pardon until he asks for it."

Kurvenal leaves to carry her message to his master.

Quickly Isolde tells Brangaene of her plan. She will pretend to make peace with Tristan, and they will drink together. She commands Brangaene, "Prepare the drink from the vial I showed you."

Tristan enters. Isolde pretends to be calm as she greets him. She asks why he has avoided her during the voyage.

"It is the custom," he answers, "that before marriage, the bride-bringer goes not near the bride."

There is another custom, she says—that enemies must join in a drink of truce before they can become friends.

"But we are enemies no longer," he replies.

There is still a feud between them, she says, because she once vowed vengeance on the slayer of Morold.

"If you loved Morold so," says Tristan, "take my sword and avenge yourself."

She refuses his sword. She proposes instead that they end the feud by drinking together.

Brangaene fearfully prepares the potion. Isolde offers it to Tristan. He drinks until she seizes the cup and drinks after him. They stand gazing into each other's eyes. Death does not come. The drink Brangaene prepared was the potion of love.

Land is near. A castle is in sight. Men on board are shouting, "Hail, King Mark!"

Tristan and Isolde are unconscious of all that is happening about them. They are lost in their love for each other.

Brangaene steps between them. Kurvenal enters and tells Tristan that the king is coming aboard to meet his bride.

As trumpets sound on shore, the curtain falls.

Act II takes place on a summer night in the garden outside King Mark's castle. At one side are steps leading up to Isolde's room. A torch burns near the door. Brangaene stands on the steps, watching the king and his hunting party, who have just left the castle.

Isolde comes from her room. She is impatient to meet Tristan. He is waiting to come into the garden when King Mark and the rest of the hunters are gone. Brangaene can still hear the hunting horns. The men are not far away, she tells Isolde. But Isolde can hear no horns. She is ready to give the signal that will bring Tristan to her.

Brangaene begs her to take care. "Blinded by love," she says, "you cannot see that a spy lurks near." That spy, she says, is Sir Melot, who pretends to be Tristan's friend.

Isolde reproves her for her suspicions. She tells the maid to signal Tristan by putting out the torch.

Brangaene continues to caution her. At last Isolde herself puts out the torch. Brangaene leaves on her way to the roof, where she is to keep watch.

Tristan comes into the garden. He and Isolde embrace rapturously. In the shelter of the night they speak of the past and of their great love—a love that will endure even after death.

From above, Brangaene has twice cautioned them that day is near. Suddenly she shrieks. Kurvenal appears and shouts a warning to Tristan.

King Mark enters with Melot and the rest of the hunting party. Melot is triumphant. The others gaze at the lovers in shocked amazement.

The kindly old king is crushed with grief. He asks how Tristan, whom he loved and trusted above all others, could have brought him such shame and sorrow.

Tristan is ready to atone with his life. He asks Isolde if she will follow him in death. She answers that even there she will follow him.

Melot draws his sword and springs forward. Tristan, seeking death, allows himself to be wounded. Kurvenal catches him as he falls.

The scene of Act III is a garden on a cliff overlooking the sea. At the back is a castle gate. On one side is a low wall. Tristan lies sleeping in the shade of a great tree. The castle is his childhood home in Brittany, where Kurvenal has brought him for safety.

The servant has sent for Isolde in the hope that she can heal Tristan as she once healed him before. A shepherd has been set to watch for her ship. Beyond the

garden he plays a mournful tune on his pipe, and presently he looks over the wall to tell Kurvenal he has not yet seen the ship. He promises that when he does, he will signal the news by playing a loud and merry tune.

Tristan wakes, crying out that he sees the ship.

Kurvenal sadly tells him there is no ship in sight.

Tristan's mind wanders. He speaks of the past and his terrible yearning for Isolde. Exhausted at last, he falls back upon his couch.

When he revives he tells of the vision that has come to him—a lovely vision of Isolde speeding toward him across the sea.

"The ship!" he cries. "Do you not see it yet?"

At that moment the shepherd is heard piping a happy tune—his signal that the ship has been sighted.

Kurvenal goes to help with the landing.

Tristan, half-crazed and wildly excited, tears the bandage from his wound and rises from his couch. Isolde hurries into the garden. He staggers to meet her. As she takes him in her arms, he cries, "Isolde!" then sinks to the ground.

She bends over him. Slowly she realizes that he is dead, and she faints beside his body.

Kurvenal has returned. The shepherd appears to tell him that another ship has landed. Kurvenal looks toward the sea. From the second ship King Mark and some of his men have come ashore. Melot is with them.

Kurvenal makes ready to defend his master's castle against them.

Brangaene's voice is heard from below, asking that the gate be opened. Melot forces his way into the garden, and Kurvenal strikes him dead.

Brangaene climbs over the wall and runs to Isolde.

King Mark enters with his soldiers. Kurvenal cannot be made to understand that they have come as friends. He fights on until he is deeply wounded. He drags himself to the feet of his dead master and dies there.

Isolde has revived.

"Hear me!" cries Brangaene. "I have told the king of the love potion and its secret."

The king tells Isolde that when he learned the lovers were not to blame, he crossed the sea to offer them his blessing.

Isolde does not hear. She is conscious only of her lover, who has gone before her in death where she must follow him. She sinks down upon his body and dies there. The grieving king blesses the dead.

# The Mastersingers of Nuremberg

Wagner was a young man when he first considered writing an opera about a German music guild of the sixteenth century. These guilds were societies made up of working people and devoted to music and poetry. From old books he learned of their rules and contests. He began sketching the story in 1845, but the libretto was not finished until 1862. Five years later the musical score was completed, and the opera was first performed in Munich on June 21, 1868.

The scene of Act I is the church of St. Katharine in Nuremberg. The choir and congregation are singing the closing hymn.

In the back of the church stands Walther von Stolzing, a young knight who is new to the city. He is gazing at a girl in the last row of seats. She is Eva, daughter of Pogner, the goldsmith. Her maid, Magdalena, is with her.

As soon as the service is over, Walther pushes his way through the crowd and asks the girl to wait.

Eva has left her kerchief on the church bench. She sends Magdalena after it. While the maid is gone, Walther speaks: "Forgive my boldness, but there is something I must know—"

Magdalena returns with the kerchief, and he is interrupted.

But Eva has also left her buckle on the bench. Magdalena goes for it, and Walther continues. The question he must ask is a matter of life and death to him.

Magdalena brings the buckle. But now she finds that she herself has forgotten something—her hymn book. As she goes back to the bench, Walther asks Eva the all-important question—is she or is she not promised to anyone in marriage?

Magdalena has already returned, and she takes it on herself to answer the young man. Eva is promised in marriage, although the bridegroom's name is not yet known. She will marry the mastersinger who wins the song contest tomorrow.

Eva asks him anxiously if he is not a mastersinger. Forgetting her reserve, she assures him that no matter who wins the contest, she will choose him and no one else.

Young David comes into the church. He is an apprentice to one of the mastersingers, Hans Sachs, the shoe-

maker. He is there to prepare the stage for a meeting of
the masters.

David is in love with Magdalena. Before she leads Eva
away, the maid asks him to instruct the knight so that
he may enter the contest.

More apprentices enter and help arrange the benches.

David explains the rules of the contest to Walther.
First he must sing a trial song before the masters, and
they must judge him worthy before he can compete.

The rules are many and complicated. Walther begins
to despair. David and the other apprentices are scornful
of the young knight who hopes to become a master in a
single day.

Two of the mastersingers enter—Pogner and Beckmesser. The pompous and elderly Beckmesser is quite
sure he will win tomorrow's contest. He is not so sure
of winning Eva's hand. One of the rules is that the girl
need not marry the contest winner if he is not pleasing
to her. However, if she refuses the winner, she shall
marry no one.

Beckmesser plans to sing to Eva alone tonight in the
hope that he may win her heart with his song. Meanwhile, Walther has told Pogner that he wishes to become
a mastersinger. Pogner is pleased, but Beckmesser is
contemptuous of the young man.

By this time all twelve of the mastersingers have gathered, including Hans Sachs, the shoemaker.

Sachs thinks that Eva and the people should judge the contest and choose the winner. He is voted down by the others. They have no faith in the people's judgment.

Pogner introduces Walther.

The young knight admits that he has not learned poetry and singing according to the rules of the guild, but he *has* learned from nature and from Sir Walther von der Vogelweide.

Hans Sachs is familiar with the name. "A good master," he says.

Walther is asked to sing a trial song. Beckmesser stands by as marker, ready to mark down any faults.

Walther chooses to sing of love and springtime. The song is interrupted again and again by the squeak of Beckmesser's chalk as he marks down faults on his slate.

When the song is over, Beckmesser declares the singer disqualified. Most of the other masters agree. Only Hans Sachs speaks a word in Walther's favor. Although the song did not follow the rules, he found it new and free and masterly.

The meeting breaks up in confusion, and Walther walks angrily off the stage. The apprentices make a game of the uproar and begin to dance.

All the masters leave except Hans Sachs. He looks thoughtfully at Walther's empty chair. Then the apprentices carry off the chair, and he turns away with a gesture that is half humorous, half indignant.

The scene of Act II is a street in Nuremberg. An alley winds toward the back. At the front, across the alley from each other, are two houses—the simple house of Hans Sachs and the grand one of Pogner.

It is a summer evening. David is outside Sachs' house, closing the shutters for the night. Other apprentices are doing the same outside other houses.

Magdalena comes out of Pogner's house, bringing David a basket of food. She is eager to know how Walther fared in his trial before the mastersingers, and she asks David for news.

The trial went badly, he tells her. Walther has been disqualified.

She is so upset that she leaves without giving him his basket of food. The other apprentices tease him because his sweetheart has carried off his supper. He is fast losing his temper, when Sachs comes up the alley and the boys run away. David and his master go into the house.

Pogner and his daughter come up the alley. He has told her nothing about Walther's trial song, and she hesitates to ask.

Pogner goes inside. Eva stays behind for a word with Magdalena, who has come to the door.

The maid tells her what she has heard—that Walther has been turned down by the mastersingers.

"What shall I do!" cries Eva.

She thinks of her old friend, Hans Sachs. Perhaps he can help her, she tells Magdalena.

There is a light in the shop across the alley. David, who is an apprentice shoemaker as well as an apprentice singer, is at work there. Sachs comes into the shop and sends him off to bed.

Alone, the shoemaker looks out into the summer night, still thinking of Walther's song. It could no more be made to fit a rule than the song of a bird, yet it was hauntingly beautiful.

Eva comes to the door. She asks about Walther's trial song.

The trial was a disaster, answers Sachs. All the knight's hopes of winning the prize are gone.

At once she believes the shoemaker is Walther's enemy. Indignantly she leaves, and Sachs, who secretly loves her, looks after her with sympathy and understanding. He knows now that she loves the young knight. "I thought as much," he says. "Now help must come."

In front of the Pogner house, Magdalena and Eva are talking. "Beckmesser told me this," says the maid. "He means to call you to your window tonight to sing you a song that will win your love."

"Must I bear that, too!" says Eva.

Pogner calls them in. Magdalena goes, but Eva has just seen Walther in the alley, and she runs to meet him.

She loves him, she says, no matter what the judgment of the mastersingers may be.

Since he has been barred from tomorrow's contest, they have only one choice left, he tells her. They must elope tonight.

The nightwatchman comes up the alley. Eva slips into the house, while Walther hides under the linden tree in the Pogner yard.

In his shop, Hans Sachs has overheard the lovers. He feels that an elopement would not be wise, and he decides to keep the two from running away.

The nightwatchman goes by. Eva comes out of the house. She has disguised herself in Magdalena's dress. As she and Walther start down the alley, Sachs opens his window so that a bright patch of light falls across their path.

They draw back. The alley is their only way of escape. If they go in the opposite direction the nightwatchman will be sure to see them.

While they hesitate, Beckmesser appears and stops under Eva's window.

Eva tells Walther, "He'll sing a song and leave." While they wait, they hide in the shadow of the linden tree.

Hans Sachs opens his door, letting the light shine out into the street. He begins to work at his bench, hammering and singing loudly.

Beckmesser is annoyed at the interruption. He asks Sachs why he is working so late.

Sachs answers that he is finishing the shoes for Beckmesser to wear tomorrow.

"The devil take the shoes!" says Beckmesser, but Sachs continues to hammer and sing.

Beckmesser says at last, "Listen to my song and give me your help, so that I may win the prize."

Sachs answers that he would rather keep working.

They come to an agreement. Sachs will listen to the song. For each fault he finds, he will strike a nail with his hammer.

Beckmesser begins his song, accompanying himself on his lute. The shoemaker marks faults with his hammer— so many faults that the shoes are finished before the song.

The noise arouses David. He sees Magdalena at Eva's window and thinks Beckmesser has come to serenade the maid. In a fit of jealousy the apprentice goes into the alley and attacks Beckmesser with a club.

The commotion attracts the other mastersingers and apprentices on the street. People come out of their houses, and the fight spreads.

Walther draws his sword and tries to force a way through the alley for Eva and himself.

Hans Sachs makes a dash from his door, catches hold of Walther, and pushes him into the shop. He shoves Eva up the steps of her own house, and Pogner takes her inside.

Women have come to their windows with basins, cans, and jugs and are pouring water down on the battling mob. The nightwatchman blows his horn. The rioters scatter in all directions.

When the watchman arrives, he comes upon a scene of peace and quiet, and he walks slowly along in the calm summer moonlight.

Act III opens the next morning in Hans Sachs' workshop. Sachs is sitting in an armchair.

David enters and sets a basket down on the workbench. It contains peace offerings from Magdalena—flowers, ribbons, a sausage, and a cake. Although she has forgiven him for his part in last night's riot, the apprentice fears his master is still angry.

But Sachs is mild and kindly. He sends David away to dress for the day's festivities.

His thoughts are still on the battle of the night before —the world is mad, he thinks, but he hopes to lead the way from folly to nobler works.

Walther comes into the shop. He has spent the night in Hans Sachs' home, and he tells the shoemaker of a dream he has had. Sachs asks him to tell his dream in the form of a song. Walther sings of his vision—a garden where a beautiful woman pointed out to him the tree of life.

Sachs writes the song as Walther sings. After the second verse, Walther cannot go on. Sachs assures him the ending will come at the proper time and place. He tells the young man to dress for the festival, and he leads him into another room.

Beckmesser comes limping in. He has suffered from the effects of last night's beating. He sees the paper on which Sachs has written Walther's song. Immediately he thinks the shoemaker has prepared the song for the contest. He slips the paper into his pocket.

When Sachs returns, Beckmesser accuses him of secretly planning to enter the contest.

The shoemaker is bewildered. Then he sees that the song is missing, and he realizes what Beckmesser is thinking.

Sachs makes it plain to him that he has no idea of entering the contest or trying to win Eva's hand. He even tells Beckmesser he may have the song to do with as he wishes.

Beckmesser is overjoyed. A song by Sachs, he thinks, must be a work of genius. If it were sung in the contest, it would be certain to win.

He embraces the shoemaker and hurries away. Sachs looks after him, reflecting that Beckmesser will help his plans along.

Eva comes to the shop. She pretends the new shoes that Sachs has made for her are pinching her feet. Actually she has come for word of Walther.

He appears, richly dressed. He and Eva gaze on each other, and now he is inspired to sing the final verse of his song.

David brings Magdalena into the shop. Sachs tells them that a mastersong has just been born and must be christened. He wishes David to witness the christening. "But as no apprentice may be a witness," he says, "I will make a master of him now."

David kneels. The shoemaker gives him a box on the ear. This is the ceremony by which an apprentice becomes a master.

The closing scene shows a meadow outside Nuremberg, where people have come for the festival. Eva takes the place of honor on the platform. The mastersingers range themselves before her.

Beckmesser has been furtively studying the new song. Because he is the oldest contestant, he is called first to sing.

Nervously he steps to the small mound in front of the platform. With no true understanding of the song, he begins to sing.

The listeners are puzzled. They whisper to one another, "How strange!"

Beckmesser blunders on, making such a spectacle of himself that the crowd breaks into laughter. In rage he leaves the mound.

"That song of mine," he shouts, "it was Sachs who wrote it!" He accuses the shoemaker of having tricked him into singing this worthless stuff.

Sachs answers quietly that Beckmesser is mistaken. He denies having written the song. "I do not boast that I wrote it," he says, "or that I can ever write a song as nobly fine as this."

"Fine?" cry the other mastersingers. "That senseless trash?"

Sachs insists the song will sound quite different when rightly sung. He calls Walther from the crowd.

The knight steps to the mound. He sings his song.

The listeners are spellbound. The masters rise in tribute. All are agreed that there will be no further contest. Walther has won the master's crown.

Eva places the victor's wreath upon his head. Both of them kneel before her father. He gives them his blessing and offers Walther a golden chain hung with medals. It is the chain presented to those who have reached the rank of mastersinger.

Walther remembers how the masters behaved toward him the day before. He refuses the chain.

The masters are perplexed. They appeal to Sachs. He takes Walther's hand and asks him not to scorn the guild. The masters have done a great service in keeping the people's art alive, and they have tried to do their work truthfully and honestly.

In a gesture of respect and reverence, Eva takes the wreath she has given Walther and places it on the head of Hans Sachs. Sachs takes the golden chain from Pogner and hangs it about Walther's neck.

Pogner kneels before the old shoemaker, the other masters raise their hands to him, and all the people assembled lift their voices in praise of their beloved chief.

# Parsifal

Wagner's last opera was a long time maturing in the mind of the composer. He became interested in the subject—the story of Parsifal, Knight of the Holy Grail, which dates from the Middle Ages—when he was a young man living in Paris, but twenty years passed before he began work on the opera.

He sketched the libretto in 1865, but did not complete it until 1877. Between 1877 and 1879 he composed the score. *Parsifal* had its first performance in Bayreuth on July 26, 1882.

The opening scene is a deep forest on a mountain in Spain. In the background is a lake. To the left is the road to Monsalvat Castle.

At Monsalvat the Holy Grail is guarded by a brotherhood of knights. The Grail is the cup from which Christ drank at the last supper. Only the pure in heart may join the brotherhood, and their nearness to the sacred cup gives them miraculous powers for good.

Also in the company are esquires, young men who attend the knights. When the curtain rises it is daybreak, and two of the esquires are sleeping under a tree. Gurnemanz, an elderly knight, is sleeping near them. He wakes and rouses the young men. He orders them to prepare the bath for King Amfortas.

Two knights enter. They tell Gurnemanz that Amfortas is still in agony. An herb brought by one of the knights has not relieved the pain of his wound.

The old man shakes his head. It is useless, he says, to try to heal the king with herbs, when only one thing and one person can be of help.

The other knights ask him what he means, but he does not answer.

They see a woman riding through the woods. She leaps from her horse and staggers toward them. She is a strange, wild figure in a robe with a snakeskin girdle. Her black hair hangs loosely, her eyes are dark and piercing.

The men know her as Kundry, a half-mad creature often seen in the forest. She gives Gurnemanz a vial of balsam for the king. If it will not heal his wound, she says, there is nothing else in Arabia that can bring him relief.

Other knights and esquires enter. Some of them are bearing King Amfortas on a litter. He hopes the water of the lake may relieve his pain, although he knows, as Gurnemanz does, that healing can come only from the deliverer who has been promised to him. This deliverer he knows only as a fool made wise by pity.

Gurnemanz gives him the balsam Kundry has brought. Amfortas thanks the girl for her devotion. She is resting, stretched out on the ground. She answers sullenly that she wants no thanks and tells him to be off to the bath.

The litter-bearers carry him away. Some of the esquires look at Kundry with suspicion. She may be a witch, they say, who wishes to harm the king.

Gurnemanz reminds them that she has been a faithful messenger and has never offered them harm.

The esquires insist that she hates them all. Besides, she is a heathen and must surely be under a curse.

Gurnemanz admits that she is a mysterious creature. Old Titurel, who built the castle, found her long ago, lying unconscious in the forest. Lately Gurnemanz has found her in a similar state.

"It was at the time when the evil one brought disgrace upon our heads," he says.

The evil one is Klingsor, a knight who wished to become a guardian of the Grail. Because of his wickedness he was barred from the brotherhood.

In revenge he turned to sorcery. He created a garden inhabited by beautiful women who preyed on the Grail knights and tried to capture them.

When Titurel grew old, his son, Amfortas, became king. Amfortas went forth with the sacred spear to destroy the enchantment of the garden. This is the spear with which Christ was wounded at the time of the crucifixion.

Klingsor employed one of the women to cast a spell over Amfortas. Then, while the king was helpless, Klingsor stole the spear and wounded him with it.

This is the shame that has come to Monsalvat. Not only has the sacred spear fallen into enemy hands, but no cure has been found for the king's wound.

While Amfortas prayed for help, a message came to him in a holy vision: "Await the blameless fool made wise through pity."

As Gurnemanz finishes the story, shouts come from the direction of the lake. A wounded swan flutters into sight, followed by knights and esquires.

"Shameful!" cry the men. "Who shot the swan?"

Other knights enter, pushing a young man forward. He readily admits that he has shot the swan. To him this is no crime.

"The animals in this forest are tame, and they come to us as friends," says Gurnemanz. "The swan was our friend. Now he lies dying."

The young man has listened with growing pity. Suddenly he breaks his bow and throws away his arrows.

Gurnemanz questions him. From where has he come? What is his name? The young man does not know.

Kundry has been listening. She eyes the young man keenly, then in a harsh voice she supplies some of the answers Gurnemanz has been seeking. Before the young man was born, she says, his father was killed in battle. Fearing her son might die in the same way, the mother brought him up in a desert, shut away from the rest of the world, where he could learn nothing of weapons.

The stranger recalls that once he saw a troupe of horsemen who fascinated him so that he ran after them. He could not overtake them, and he lost his way. He wandered on and on with the bow and arrows he had made to protect himself from men and beasts.

Again Kundry speaks. "Robbers and giants learned to fear him in combat."

The stranger is surprised. "Who fears me?" he asks.

"The wicked," she answers.

"Those who fought me—were they wicked?" he asks. "Who is good?"

Gurnemanz laughs at the young man's innocence, then he becomes serious again. "Your mother must grieve for you," he says.

"She grieves no more," says Kundry. "His mother is dead."

"It is false!" cries the stranger.

"As I rode by, I saw her dying, fool," says Kundry, "and she sent you her greeting."

The young man seizes Kundry by the throat. Gurnemanz pulls him away from her. "Are you mad, boy?" he says. "Kundry spoke the truth. She never lies."

The stranger begins to tremble. "I am fainting!" he gasps.

Kundry runs to a spring in the woods and brings him water. Gurnemanz thanks her for her goodness. "I never do good!" she says. She creeps away among the bushes, muttering that she wishes she could sleep and never waken.

Across the lake esquires and knights appear, carrying Amfortas home, and Gurnemanz helps the stranger slowly along toward the castle.

The scene changes to a hall in Monsalvat, where tables are laid for the holy feast. The Grail knights come forward. Bearers enter, carrying the wounded king. Before them march four esquires bearing the covered shrine of the Grail.

The king is helped to a couch. The shrine is placed before him.

Old Titurel, Amfortas' father, cries out from a room beyond the hall. Must he die, he asks, before the deliverer comes?

Amfortas begs his father to take office once more.

Titurel replies that he is too feeble and old. Amfortas must serve and atone for his guilt. "Reveal the Grail!" orders the old man.

The esquires uncover the shrine. Amfortas bows be-

fore the crystal cup. The hall grows dim. A beam of light falls from above, and the Grail shines with a wine-red glow.

Amfortas lifts the cup and waves it slowly from side to side, thus blessing the holy feast.

He puts the Grail down. The glow fades from it, and the hall grows light again.

The knights take their places at the table. Gurnemanz has kept a place empty beside him, and he beckons the stranger to come to the table, but the young man stands motionless.

Amfortas takes no part in the feast. He lies on the couch, suffering agony, until the bearers carry him away. Knights and esquires follow until only Gurnemanz and the stranger are left.

The stranger is deeply moved by the king's suffering.

Gurnemanz asks him, "Do you know what you have seen?"

The stranger shakes his head.

Gurnemanz says in irritation, "Then you are nothing but a fool!" and he pushes the young man out of the hall.

The second act begins in the tower of Klingsor's castle. Klingsor is sitting before a magic mirror which shows him other parts of his domain. He sees the stranger drawing near.

Calling on his magical powers, he summons Kundry. She comes before him in a strange blue light.

He reproaches her for having gone to the Grail knights, who look on her as no better than a beast. He reminds her that it was she who trapped Amfortas and caused him to lose the sacred spear. Now the fool is on his way, and she must bind him in her spell.

"I will not!" she cries. "You cannot force me!"

Yet even as she speaks, she knows he holds her in his power.

Klingsor looks down from the tower and commands his men to attack the stranger. He watches the battle and describes it to Kundry. The stranger has met Klingsor's knights fearlessly. He has snatched a weapon from one of them and is beating them back.

Klingsor laughs at the defeat of his "heroes," for whom

he has only contempt. He sends Kundry to trap the stranger.

The tower sinks out of sight. The magic garden rises in its place.

Flower-maidens, dressed in many-colored veils, are running about, alarmed by the confusion of the battle. Looking at the stranger, they ask one another, "Who is our foe?"

He comes farther into the garden, gazing in childish delight. The maidens' fear changes to wonder, their wonder to pleasure.

Some of them slip away and come back dressed as flowers. Soon all the maidens are decked out in flower costumes. They surround the stranger and quarrel over him until he shouts, "Begone!" and tries to escape.

A voice comes to him. It is Kundry, calling, "Parsifal!"

"Parsifal?" he repeats, and he remembers the name as his own.

Kundry sends the maidens away.

Parsifal looks about him. Through an opening in a hedge he sees Kundry lying on a couch of flowers. Under Klingsor's enchantment, she is young and beautiful.

She tells him of his mother—how the poor woman grieved herself to death when he left and never returned.

Parsifal is filled with sorrow and repentance. She speaks consolingly. His mother, she tells him, entrusted her with a kiss for him, and she presses her lips to his.

He starts to his feet.

"Amfortas!" he exclaims. "The spear-wound—it burns in my heart!"

For the first time he knows the meaning of sin, and now he understands the suffering of the king. Once he stood before the Holy Grail, he heard heaven's call. "But I, the fool, fled here to deeds of childish folly!" he cries.

Kundry tries to turn his thoughts back to her.

He looks into her face. With the new understanding that has come to him, he knows it was she who caused the king to be wounded and the sacred sword to be stolen.

"Destroyer!" he exclaims.

She asks for his pity, all the while striving to cast her spell upon him.

He promises her love and salvation if she will show him the way back to Amfortas. She refuses. She calls to Klingsor. He comes over the wall. "The fool shall fall by his master's spear!" he shouts, and he hurls the sacred spear.

But the weapon does not strike. It hangs in midair over Parsifal's head. Parsifal grasps it.

With the spear he makes the sign of the cross. The castle falls in ruins. The garden withers. Kundry falls to the ground.

Parsifal pauses on top of the ruined wall. "You know where you may find me," he tells her.

She raises her head, looking after him as he leaves her.

The third act opens at the edge of the forest near Monsalvat Castle. In the forest is a spring, with a hermit's hut nearby.

Gurnemanz comes out of the hut. Years have passed, and he has grown very old. He stands listening. It is Good Friday, and the quiet peace of the morning has been broken by groans and cries.

He goes toward the sounds and finds Kundry unconscious in a thicket. He revives her. She looks up at him, the wildness gone from her gaze.

"Have you no word for me?" he asks.

She answers brokenly that she wishes to be of service.

There is little for her to do, he says. The brotherhood of knights is all but disbanded.

She sees someone in the forest. Silently she points, then goes into the hut.

Parsifal enters slowly and uncertainly. He wears a suit of black armor.

He puts down his weapons. One of them is the sacred sword.

He tells Gurnemanz of his long struggle to find his way back to King Amfortas. He came through many dangers. Not once did he use the spear in battle, but he guarded it and kept it sacred.

Gurnemanz tells him of the sorrow that has come to the Knights of the Grail. Amfortas, crazed by suffering, will no longer serve his holy office. The shrine of the Grail remains closed, and old Titurel, the former king, is dead.

Parsifal blames himself for the woes of the brotherhood. Although he was chosen to deliver the knights from misfortune, he has failed them.

He allows Gurnemanz and Kundry to lead him to the spring, where they help him remove his armor. Kundry bathes his feet. Gurnemanz sprinkles water on Parsifal's head.

Kundry takes from her bosom a golden vial of balm. She pours part of it on Parsifal's feet and dries them with her hair. Gurnemanz pours the rest of the balm over Parsifal's head and blesses him.

Parsifal sprinkles a handful of water over Kundry's head. "Be you baptized, and trust in the Redeemer," he says.

Looking across the sunlit fields and forest, he loses himself in their beauty. The beauty is the spell of Good Friday, says Gurnemanz.

Kundry looks earnestly into Parsifal's face, and he gently kisses her forehead.

Gurnemanz brings his mantle from the hut, and he and Kundry place it about Parsifal's shoulders. Parsifal takes up the spear, and the three leave together.

The scene changes to a hall in the castle. Knights enter, bearing Titurel's coffin. Others bring Amfortas into the hall. In front of the king are four esquires carrying the shrine of the Grail.

The knights urge Amfortas to perform his kingly office and uncover the Grail. He refuses. Weeping before the body of his father, he prays that he, too, may die. Wildly he calls upon the knights to slay him. When he has given his life for his sins, he says, the Grail will shine again.

Parsifal, Gurnemanz, and Kundry have entered. Parsifal moves forward. He extends the spear and touches its point to Amfortas' side.

The king's face lights with rapture. Miraculously his wound is healed, and his suffering is ended.

"Be whole, purified, and atoned," says Parsifal, "for I now hold your office. Blessed be your suffering, for it has given the power of pity and understanding to the timid fool."

He raises the spear. "This I bring back to you," he says.

He orders the esquires to uncover the shrine. They obey, and the Grail shines with a soft radiance.

The knights join in a prayer of thanksgiving. A white dove flies low over Parsifal's head. Kundry has been gazing up at him. Now she sinks lifeless at his feet.

Amfortas and Gurnemanz kneel, as Parsifal slowly waves the Grail in benediction.

# Rigoletto

Giuseppe Verdi was already a leading Italian composer when he composed *Rigoletto* in 1850. Victor Hugo's play, *The King Amuses Himself*, furnished the story.

At that time part of Italy was ruled by Austria. Before the opera was written, Austrian censors decided the libretto was not fit to be given in public. The story dealt with the wickedness of a French king. The authorities believed such an opera would appear to criticize the Austrian royalty, and they feared anything that might stir the Italians to revolt.

Verdi refused to give up the idea. The situation was at a deadlock, when the police commissioner of Venice, who admired Verdi's operas, came forward with a plan. He suggested that the French king in the story be changed to an Italian duke.

Verdi agreed to this and a few smaller changes. He

enthusiastically set to work on the music and finished the score in forty days. *Rigoletto* was first performed in Venice on March 11, 1851.

The setting of the opera is Mantua, in northern Italy, during the sixteenth century. The curtain rises on a brilliantly lighted room in the palace of the duke. Doorways open into other rooms where ladies and gentlemen are dancing.

The duke of Mantua enters. He is telling his friend, Borsa, about a beautiful girl he has seen lately. He often disguises himself and wanders about in search of adventure. It was on one of these excursions that he first saw the girl. He does not know her name, but he followed her and knows where she lives.

The next moment he is admiring the wife of Count Ceprano, a gentleman of the court. "This one or that one," he says. One love means no more to him than another.

Rigoletto, the hunchbacked jester, has come in. Hated by the courtiers, he is under the duke's protection, and they have no defense against his sharp wit and cruel tongue.

As the duke leads Countess Ceprano away, Rigoletto taunts her husband.

Count Ceprano goes out after his wife. The jester follows.

Marullo, one of the courtiers, tells the others of a

discovery he has made. The humpbacked jester has a sweetheart hidden away in another part of the city.

Rigoletto and the duke return. Rigoletto's manner is so insulting that the courtiers are aroused. Even the duke warns him that some day he may go too far.

There is a disturbance outside. Old Count Monterone enters and denounces the duke for the dishonor of his daughter. Rigoletto jeers at the old man.

Monterone calls down a terrible curse on both the duke and his jester. Undisturbed, the duke orders the old man off to prison, but Rigoletto is struck with sudden fear.

The next scene is the street outside Rigoletto's house. The jester is on his way home, still thinking of the curse.

Out of the night comes a stranger wrapped in a long dark cloak. He is Sparafucile, a professional assassin. "Can I serve you?" he asks. "Can I rid you of an enemy or a rival?"

Rigoletto answers that he has no need of him now. "But if I should need you, where can you be found?" he asks.

"Here, every evening," says Sparafucile.

He leaves, and Rigoletto tells himself, "We are alike. He stabs with his sword, I with my tongue."

He cries out against the fate that made him an ugly, twisted creature, fit for nothing but to be a laughing-stock. He thinks of the duke and the courtiers who make sport of him, and he bursts out in fury, "How I hate you!"

He unlocks the door in the wall and lets himself into his courtyard. A girl comes out to meet him. She is not Rigoletto's sweetheart, as the courtiers suppose, but his daughter, Gilda.

She is his only joy. His greatest fear is that harm might come to her. She knows nothing of his life away from her. He has shielded her from the evil of the duke's court.

In the three months since she came here, Gilda has been out only to morning church services. Again he forbids her to wander about the city, and he calls Giovanna, the old woman he has set to watch over her.

"Is the terrace always locked?" he asks.

The old woman assures him that it is.

He hears a sound outside. He opens the door in the wall, goes out, and looks up and down the street.

While the door is open, a man slips into the courtyard. It is the duke in disguise. He bribes Giovanna to be quiet, and he hides behind a tree.

Rigoletto returns. He cautions the old woman never to open the door to anyone, and he takes leave of Gilda.

The duke overhears their conversation. Now he knows that the girl is Rigoletto's daughter.

The jester leaves. Gilda confesses to Giovanna that her conscience troubles her. She has not told her father about the young man who follows her when she goes to church.

Her father would only put an end to the matter, says Giovanna, and she asks, "Would that please you?"

"Oh, no!" says Gilda.

The duke comes out of hiding. Gilda recognizes him as the young man who has been following her. Giovanna leaves them alone together.

The duke swears his love for the girl. When she asks his name, he tells her he is Walter Maldè, a poor student.

Giovanna comes to warn them that she has heard someone in the street. Gilda fears her father has come home. The duke runs into the house. Giovanna follows to let him out through the terrace door.

"Walter Maldè!" repeats Gilda, and she stands for a while in the courtyard, lost in a dream of love. She goes into the house and comes out on the terrace, gazing in the direction the young man has gone.

A group of courtiers gather in the street outside. Ceprano, Borsa, and Marullo are among them. All are armed and masked.

They spy on Gilda. When she goes back into the house, they tell one another that she is the one they are seeking—Rigoletto's mysterious sweetheart.

Rigoletto appears. The courtiers tell him they have come to play a joke on Ceprano, whose house is across the street. They are going to carry off his wife.

Rigoletto willingly joins them.

Marullo places a mask on him. At the same time he slips a handkerchief over the jester's eyes.

Unable to see, Rigoletto holds a ladder beneath his own terrace, thinking the men are climbing the wall of Ceprano's house. The courtiers break into the house. They quickly return, carrying Gilda, whom they have bound and gagged.

They are gone before Rigoletto discovers his eyes are bandaged. He tears off the mask.

The courtiers have left a lantern behind. By its light he sees a scarf in the street. It is Gilda's scarf.

Now he realizes how he has been tricked, and he falls to the ground with a cry of anguish.

Act II takes place in a room of the palace. It is the next morning. The duke enters, disturbed because Gilda has disappeared.

The courtiers come in with their story of how they tricked Rigoletto into helping kidnap his own sweetheart.

"It must be my lost one!" says the duke. He asks where they have taken her.

"We brought her here," they tell him, and he hurries away to her.

Rigoletto enters. He tries to pretend that nothing is wrong. All the time he is looking for some sign of Gilda. The courtiers watch, enjoying his misery.

At last he demands the girl they carried away from his house.

"If you've lost a sweetheart," they tell him, "look for her somewhere else."

"She is my daughter," says Rigoletto. "Give her back to me."

He starts toward the next room. The courtiers bar his way. He storms at them. He pleads.

Gilda comes out of the next room and runs to her father's arms.

"Why are you weeping?" he asks.

Pathetically she tells him how the duke has deceived her.

Old Monterone passes through the room on the way to his prison cell. He sees the duke's portrait on the wall. "This evil man is still unpunished," he says. "My curse was in vain."

"No!" cries Rigoletto. "Vengeance is near!"

Act III takes place at night in a lonely spot near a river. In the background are the towers of Mantua. On one side is an old inn with a stairway leading to a loft. Inside sits Sparafucile, the assassin. Outside are Gilda and her father.

Rigoletto promises her that she shall have revenge on the duke.

"I love him," says Gilda, and she believes that in spite of his deceit the duke loves her.

Rigoletto leads her to the inn where they can look through a crack in the wall. They see the duke enter. Tonight he is disguised as a cavalry officer.

He asks for a room and some wine. While Sparafucile goes to bring the wine, the duke expresses his opinion of women. They are changeable as a feather in the wind, he says, yet pursuing them is the only joy worth knowing.

Sparafucile's sister, Maddalena, comes down the stairs. Leaving the duke with her, Sparafucile steps outside. He speaks to Rigoletto, "Your man is here. Shall I put an end to him now or later?"

"Later," says Rigoletto, and Sparafucile goes away.

Inside the inn, the duke is already making love to Maddalena.

Outside, Rigoletto and Gilda watch and listen. Is she convinced, he asks, that the duke is false? Gilda, weeping, replies that her heart is broken.

Rigoletto orders her to go home, disguise herself as a man, and go to Verona, where he will meet her.

After she has gone, he summons Sparafucile from behind the inn.

Rigoletto pays the assassin ten pieces of gold. He agrees to pay an equal sum at midnight, after the duke has been murdered.

Rigoletto leaves, and Sparafucile goes back into the inn. He shows the duke upstairs to his room. The duke lies down and falls asleep.

A storm is rising, with distant thunder and lightning, as Gilda returns. She has dressed herself as a man, but she could not obey the rest of her father's command. She has come to be near the duke.

Sparafucile and his sister are discussing the man upstairs. Maddalena has fallen in love with him. She asks that he be spared, until Sparafucile promises, "If another man comes to the inn before midnight, he shall die instead."

Listening outside, Gilda resolves to save the duke, even though it costs her life.

She knocks at the inn. She enters. The door closes behind her.

The storm begins to die, and the rain stops. Rigoletto appears outside the inn. A clock strikes midnight, and he knocks at the door.

Sparafucile comes out, dragging a sack. Rigoletto pays him ten more gold pieces. Sparafucile delivers the sack and disappears into the inn.

While Rigoletto is taking the sack to the river, a voice comes to him. In the upper room, the duke is singing!

Horrified, Rigoletto tears open the sack and looks on the face of his daughter. Her dying words are a plea for his forgiveness.

"Ah, the curse!" he cries, and he falls in a faint beside her body.

# Il Trovatore

Il Trovatore ("The Troubadour") is based on a drama, *El Trovador,* by the Spanish playwright, Gutiérrez. Verdi composed the opera in 1852. It was first performed in Rome on January 19, 1853, with tremendous success.

The setting of the opera is fifteenth-century Spain. The scene of Act I is the royal palace. Count di Luna has apartments there. Also a member of the palace household is Lady Leonora, an attendant to the queen.

The count loves Leonora and is wildly jealous of her. Lately a troubadour has been stealing into the palace garden to serenade her. Each night the count waits under her window, hoping to capture the intruder, and he has posted a guard to keep watch in the hall outside his apartments.

Ferrando, the count's personal servant, comes into

the hall and finds the soldiers and servants dozing. They ask him to tell them a story to keep them awake while they stand guard.

Ferrando obliges with the story of old Count di Luna, father of the present count. The old count had two sons. When the younger one was a baby, the nurse woke one morning to find a gypsy woman bending over the cradle. The nurse called for help. The gypsy swore she meant no harm, but only wished to tell the baby's fortune. Nevertheless, she was beaten and driven away.

After that day the baby grew sickly. The count believed the woman had put a curse on his son, and he sentenced her to be burned at the stake.

The gypsy left a daughter, Azucena, who had a child of her own. To avenge her mother's death, Azucena kidnapped the count's baby. Later the bones of a child were found in the ashes about the stake where the gypsy woman had been burned. It was widely believed that Azucena had thrown the count's child into the fire.

Ferrando still hopes to track her down. Although many years have passed, he is certain he would recognize her.

The old count refused to believe his child was dead. As he lay dying, he ordered his other son, who is now Count di Luna, never to stop searching for the brother who was kidnapped.

The clock strikes midnight. Wide awake now, the shuddering servants and soldiers return to their posts.

The next scene takes place in the garden. It is night, with clouds across the moon. Leonora comes down the stairs from the palace. Her friend, Inez, follows and tries to persuade her to come back inside, but Leonora waits, hoping the troubadour will come.

She tells Inez of her first meeting with him. It was at a tournament. One of the knights wore black armor, and no one knew who he was. He was winner in every contest, and she crowned him with the victory wreath.

Soon afterward the war broke out. Time passed, with no word of him. Then one night she heard his voice outside her window.

Inez warns her that this unknown troubadour had best be forgotten.

"I could never forget him. I would die for him," answers Leonora.

She and Inez climb the stairs into the palace. The Count di Luna comes into the garden. As he stands under Leonora's window, he hears the troubadour's serenade from another part of the garden.

Leonora, too, hears the song. She runs down the stairs. In the darkness she mistakes the count for her lover and throws herself into his arms.

The troubadour, watching from among the trees, cries out, "Unfaithful one!"

The moon comes from behind the clouds. Leonora recognizes both men.

"It was a mistake—I could not see!" she tells the troubadour. "I love no one but you!"

The count demands to know the intruder's name.

"I am Manrico," answers the troubadour, and he boldly shows his face.

The count is stunned. Manrico is an outlaw with a price on his head. He is fighting on the side of the rebels who are at war with the king.

Again Leonora confesses her love for the troubadour. "By these words," says the count, "you have condemned him to death!"

The men draw their swords, as the act closes.

Act II opens in a gypsy camp in the mountains. A fire burns at the back of an old hut. Azucena, the gypsy woman, is sitting by the fire. Manrico is lying near her.

Girls are dancing. Men are busy at their forges and anvils, and women are bringing them wine.

Azucena has been intent on the fire. The flames remind her of the dreadful day when her mother died at the stake. She begins to speak of it.

The other gypsies leave in search of food. When Manrico and Azucena are alone, he asks her to finish her story.

She tells him of the count who condemned her mother to death. "Before she was executed," says Azucena, "she called to me, 'Avenge my wrong!' "

"And did you avenge her?" asks Manrico.

Azucena answers that she stole the count's son and brought him to the fire where her mother had perished. For a moment she was overcome by agony and grief. When she recovered, she saw that she had thrown her own child into the flames, while the count's son lay before her.

Manrico is amazed. "Am I not your son?" he asks. "Then who am I?"

"You are my son," she answers.

"But you told me—" begins Manrico.

"Forget what I told you," she says. "Sometimes I am confused and speak foolishly. Have I not always been a mother to you? When I heard you had been killed in battle, did I not come to bury you? When I found you were alive, did I not heal your wounds?"

Manrico is proud of his wounds. He recalls the battle when he faced Count di Luna and his men alone.

"I fell," he says, "but I fell like a hero."

Azucena reminds him that once in single combat he defeated the count. "He was beneath your sword," she says, "yet you spared his life. Why did you spare him?"

Manrico does not know. "There was some strange force that would not let me strike."

"If ever again you meet in battle," says Azucena, "show him no mercy."

A messenger comes with a letter from Ruiz, a soldier in Manrico's service. Ruiz has written that the rebels have captured the fortress of Castellor, and Manrico must come to help defend it. The letter also gives word of Leonora. Believing Manrico has been killed in battle, she is about to enter a convent.

In spite of Azucena's protests, Manrico leaves.

The next scene takes place at night in a court outside the convent. Count di Luna is there with Ferrando and a group of his other followers. He has come to carry Leonora away before she can take the final vows that bind her to the church.

Leonora and Inez enter with a procession of nuns. As they move toward the chapel, the count stops them. He declares that Leonora shall never take the holy vows. "You shall be mine!" he says.

Before she can reply, Manrico appears.

She is overwhelmed at seeing the troubadour she believed dead.

Manrico's followers, led by Ruiz, pour into the court-yard, and Manrico takes Leonora away.

Act III opens in an army camp. Count di Luna's forces have gathered there to attack the fortress of Castellor. The count comes out of his tent and gazes in wrath toward Castellor, where Manrico has taken Leonora.

Ferrando enters, bringing news. A gypsy woman has been found near the camp. Some of the men suspected her of spying and took her prisoner.

Soldiers come to the count's tent, bringing Azucena

"I know her!" exclaims Ferrando. "It was she who threw your brother into the fire!"

She denies the crime. She cries in desperation, "Manrico, save me!"

"Is she the mother of Manrico?" asks the count. This is a rare stroke of fortune. Now it is in his power to avenge the death of his brother and at the same time revenge himself on Manrico.

The scene shifts to Castellor. Manrico and Leonora are together. The count's armies have surrounded the fortress.

Manrico tells Leonora not to fear, and they turn toward the chapel where a priest is waiting to perform their marriage ceremony.

Ruiz enters with word that Azucena has been taken prisoner. She is to be burned, he says, within sight of the fortress windows.

Manrico orders an attack on the count's armies. At any cost, Azucena must be saved.

But the attack fails. Manrico is captured. He and Azucena are imprisoned in the royal palace.

Act IV opens in a wing of the palace. At one corner is a tower with barred windows.

Ruiz and Leonora enter in the darkness. He shows her the tower where the prisoners are kept, and she sends him away. She has come to be near Manrico and to save him if she can.

She hears the voices of monks in a prayer for the dying. Then from the tower she hears Manrico praying that death will bring him peace.

The count enters with several of his men. Leonora hides in the shadows. The count instructs the men that the executions are to be at sunrise. Manrico shall die by the ax; Azucena shall be burned at the stake.

The count's men leave. Leonora speaks to the count. She pleads with him to spare Manrico.

He replies that no price on earth can save Manrico now.

"There is a price," says Leonora, "and I offer it. Let Manrico go free, and I am yours."

"Swear it," orders the count.

"I swear it," she says.

He calls a prison guard.

Leonora wears a ring in which she has concealed poison. While the count speaks to the guard, she sucks the poison from the ring.

"He shall have me," she says, "but cold and dead!"

The count turns back to her. "The man shall go free," he says.

The final scene is a prison cell with a window at one side and a door in the back. Azucena is lying on a pallet. Manrico sits beside her.

It is nearly time for the executions. But the finger of death is already on her forehead, says Azucena. By the time the executioners come for her, she will be dead.

Her mind wanders. She and Manrico talk of the mountain home where they once lived happily, and they pretend that some day they will return there.

She falls asleep. While Manrico kneels beside her, Leonora comes into the cell.

Manrico gives thanks to heaven. It was his greatest wish to see her again before he died.

"I am here to save you," says Leonora.

She tells him to go quickly. He refuses to go without her.

"I have promised to stay," she tells him.

He guesses that she has made a bargain with the count. Fiercely he accuses her of having sold herself.

She tells him what she has done. Already she feels the effects of the poison. She bids him farewell, sinks to the floor, and dies.

Count di Luna comes to the door. He sees how he has been tricked, and he orders his soldiers to take Manrico to the execution.

Azucena wakes and asks where Manrico has gone.

"To his death," answers the count. He drags her to the window and forces her to watch while Manrico is executed.

"He was your brother!" shrieks Azucena. "Oh, my mother, you are avenged!"

As she falls unconscious, the count cries out in horror.

# La Traviata

In 1852 Verdi visited Paris where he saw *The Lady of the Camellias,* the popular play by the younger Alexandre Dumas. It impressed him deeply, and that same year he began an opera based on the play.

The opera was *La Traviata* ("The Lost One"). Its first performance, in Venice on March 6, 1853, was a disaster. The leading tenor was hoarse. The stout prima donna cut a ridiculous figure in the role of the frail heroine. Besides, *La Traviata* was in modern dress, which was strange to audiences of that day.

The composer did not lose faith in his opera. The following year a new version, with a different cast, was given in Venice. This time it was a brilliant success.

The opening scene is in Paris in the home of Violetta Valery. She is giving one of her fashionable parties. In the group about her are Doctor Grenvil and the Marquis d'Obigny. Her friend, Flora, arrives late with Baron Duphol.

Soon afterward Gastone, another guest, arrives. He has brought his friend, Alfredo Germont, a young man from Provence, in southern France. Alfredo has long admired Violetta from a distance.

Violetta and her guests sit down to supper. Under cover of the conversation, Gastone tells her, "Alfredo thinks of you all the time."

"Nonsense!" says Violetta.

Gastone insists it is true. During her recent illness Alfredo asked about her every day.

Baron Duphol speaks up. This Alfredo annoys him, he says.

The wine has been poured. Alfredo proposes a toast, in which he is joined by Violetta and the others.

A waltz strikes up in the ballroom, and they all start off to finish the evening with dancing. A sudden faintness seizes Violetta. She sends the guests on into the ballroom. Only Alfredo stays with her.

"If you were mine, I would watch over you," he says.

She laughs at him. Then, realizing he is in earnest, she tells him she has only friendship to offer.

He goes away. The other guests come back from the ballroom and take leave of her.

Alone, she thinks of Alfredo. Could it be, she wonders, that they might find happiness together?

"What folly!" she exclaims, trying to put the thought aside. Life for her can mean nothing more than the pursuit of pleasure. She lives only to be free.

From outside comes the voice of Alfredo repeating that he has loved her since the first day he saw her.

"Folly!" she says again, and for the moment she refuses to admit the love she has begun to feel for him.

But Act II finds Alfredo and Violetta together in their country home near Paris. Alfredo enters and meditates on the happiness he has found. It is three months since she gave up her old life and came here with him. Since then, he says, he has been almost in heaven.

Annina, Violetta's maid, comes into the room. He questions her and learns that she has just been to Paris to sell her mistress' coach and horses and other possessions to help pay the expenses of this country house.

He is shocked and ashamed. He had not realized the state of affairs. He asks the maid to say nothing of their talk, and he hurries off to try to raise the money that is needed.

Violetta enters. A servant delivers a letter from Flora —an invitation to a dance. Violetta puts it indifferently aside.

The servant announces a visitor. It is Alfredo's father.

The elder Germont enters. He accuses her of leading his son to ruin and living in luxury at his expense.

She shows him papers she has drawn up. He learns

from them that she is giving all her possessions to Alfredo.

In spite of himself, Germont is impressed by her dignity and unselfishness. His bitter accusations turn to pleading.

He has a daughter, he says, who has met a man who loves her and wishes to marry her. "But how can she hope for a happy marriage," he asks, "if our family name is dishonored?"

"I understand," says Violetta. "You want me to give up Alfredo until after his sister's marriage."

No, he says, she must give up Alfredo altogether.

She refuses. "He is all I have in the world."

"It is a sacrifice, I know," says Germont, "but listen to me." He paints a picture of her future with Alfredo. Their forbidden love will bring no lasting happiness, and it will separate Alfredo from his family.

She admits that what he says may be true. After a struggle with her feelings, she consents to put Alfredo out of her life.

She sends Germont away. She writes a note, accepting Flora's invitation, and asks Annina to deliver it.

"Now I must write to *him*," she says. "What shall I say? How shall I find the strength?"

She writes the letter. Alfredo comes in.

"You are writing?" he says. "To whom?"

"To you," she answers.

He asks for the letter.

"Later," she says.

He does not insist. His mind is occupied with the angry note he has just had from his father.

"I expect him here soon," says Alfredo.

"You must talk with him alone," she says.

She bids him good-by and leaves the house.

Alfredo waits. It is growing late. He begins to think his father will not come until tomorrow.

The servant looks in to report that Violetta has just left for Paris. Shortly afterward a messenger arrives with her note.

Alfredo reads it in stunned surprise. Violetta has left him.

His father comes in from the garden.

"I know how you suffer," he says, and he begs his son to come home where peace and happiness are waiting.

Alfredo can think only of Violetta.

On the table he finds the invitation to the dance. "Ah, she will be there!" he says, and his anger rises as he thinks that she has deserted him to return to the old life.

The scene changes to a room in Flora's house. Guests are arriving for the party. For entertainment there is gambling and there are singers dressed as gypsy fortune-tellers and Spanish matadors.

Alfredo enters and joins the guests at the gambling table.

Violetta and Baron Duphol come in together. They are startled to see Alfredo, and the baron warns her jealously, "Don't speak a word to him."

At the gambling table Alfredo is having a run of good luck. "I'll win tonight," he says, "and afterward I'll go to the country to enjoy what I've won."

"Alone?" asks Flora.

"No," says Alfredo, "with the person who was with me before and then left me."

The baron starts up angrily.

"Did you speak to me?" asks Alfredo.

"You have had such good fortune," says the baron, "that I'm tempted to try my luck."

Alfredo accepts the challenge. The two men gamble at cards. Time after time Alfredo wins.

Supper is announced, and all the guests go out. As soon as the room is deserted, Violetta comes back. Alfredo follows her.

"You called me," he says coldly. "What do you want?"

She asks him to leave. The baron is a dangerous man, and she is afraid of what he may do.

"If I go, will you go with me?" he asks.

"No," she says. "I gave my word that I would not see you again."

He thinks it was the baron to whom she gave her word. In a rage, he calls in the other guests. "This woman squandered all her possessions on me," he says. "I took everything she offered. The time has come for me to clear myself of this disgrace. Witness that I have paid my debt to her!"

He takes the money he has won and flings it in her face.

The elder Germont enters. He and the others are outraged at Alfredo's public humiliation of Violetta.

Alfredo is already sorry for his outburst. Baron Duphol promises that the insult shall be punished, while Violetta tries to make Alfredo understand that she has never been unfaithful.

Act III takes place in the bedroom of Violetta's apartment in Paris. It is early morning. Violetta is asleep in bed. She is gravely ill of consumption, and Annina is caring for her.

The doctor calls. He speaks encouragingly to Violetta, but as he leaves, he whispers to Annina, "She has only a short time to live."

From the street come sounds of a Paris carnival. Violetta thinks of those who suffer in the midst of this rejoicing. She has twenty louis left, and she sends the maid out to give ten louis to the poor.

A letter has come from the elder Germont. She reads it again: "You kept your word . . . The duel took place. The baron was wounded, but is now recovering . . . I have revealed your sacrifice to Alfredo. He will come to ask your pardon. I, too, shall come."

"I wait and wait," she says, "and they do not come."

She looks in the mirror and is shocked to find herself so changed.

Annina returns and breathlessly announces that Alfredo is outside.

He enters. He and Violetta rush into each other's arms.

"Nothing can ever separate us again," he says.

They plan to leave Paris together. She will be well again. All their future will be happy.

Suddenly her strength fails. Alfredo is alarmed. Annina goes to bring the doctor.

"Why must I die so young!" cries Violetta. "Why must I die now, with happiness so near!"

Annina returns with the doctor and Alfredo's father. The elder Germont embraces Violetta.

"You have come late," she tells him. She gives Alfredo a small picture of herself. "It is for the one you may some day marry," she says.

For a little while she feels happy and free of pain. "I live again!" she cries. The next moment she is dead.

# Aida

In 1869 a new opera house was opened in Cairo to celebrate the completion of the Suez Canal. Ismail Pasha, khedive of Egypt, wanted an opera written especially for the new theater, and he approached Verdi with the idea. At first the composer was not interested, but after seeing an outline of the story, he became enthusiastic. Even before the libretto was finished, he had set to work on the music.

The opera was *Aida*. It was first performed in Cairo on Christmas Eve, 1871.

The story takes place in ancient Egypt. The opening scene is a hall in the king's palace. A gateway at the back opens on a view of the city of Memphis, with the pyramids beyond.

Ramphis, a high priest, and Radames, a young officer in the king's army, are discussing the rumors of war.

The priest says that already the goddess, Isis, has chosen a man to lead Egypt's armies. This man is young and brave, he adds, with a significant look at Radames, and he goes to take the goddess' message to the king.

Radames thinks of the glory that would be his if he could lead the Egyptian hosts to victory—glory that he could share with his beloved Aida.

Amneris, daughter of the king, enters the hall. She loves Radames, but she suspects that he and her slave girl, Aida, are in love with each other. She calls the girl to her and watches the two together for some sign of their true feelings.

The king enters with a train of priests, guards, and court officials. A messenger has just brought grave news. The Ethiopians have invaded Egypt, led by Amonasro, the warrior king.

When Aida hears the name of the Ethiopian king, she cries out. Amonasro is her father. This secret she has kept ever since she was taken prisoner and made a slave by the Egyptians.

War is declared. The king reveals that Radames has been chosen to lead the Egyptian armies.

Radames thanks the gods for his good fortune, and Amneris bids him return victorious. The others take up her words, "Return victorious!" and Radames leaves with them for a sacred ceremony in the temple of the god, Vulcan.

Aida remains behind. She asks herself how she could have joined in the cry, "Return victorious." Her father has gone to war for her, to restore her to home and country. How could she have wished Radames to conquer? Yet how can she wish defeat and death to Radames, whom she loves?

The second scene is the dimly lighted temple of Vulcan. In a solemn ceremony Radames is given a silver veil and the sacred sword. The fate of Egypt is now in his hands.

Act II opens in Amneris' apartments. The Ethiopian armies have been defeated, and the princess' slaves are helping her dress for the triumphal celebration.

Aida enters. Amneris has laid a cunning trap. She tells the slave girl that Radames has been killed.

Aida is stricken with grief.

"Look at me. I lied to you," says Amneris. "Radames lives!"

Aida cannot hide her relief. She gives thanks to heaven that Radames has been spared.

Now Amneris knows the truth. "You love him!" she cries. "I love him, too. I am your rival—I, daughter of Egypt's king!"

For a moment Aida is on the point of replying that she, too, is the daughter of a king. Then, humbling herself, she asks Amneris to have pity on her.

But there is no pity in Amneris' heart. "At the festival

you shall be my lowly slave," she tells Aida cruelly, "while I sit beside the king."

The next scene shows an entrance to the city. At one side is a temple. At the other, beneath a gorgeous canopy, is a throne. There is a gateway at the back. The avenue leading into the city is thronged with people.

The king and his attendants enter. Amneris follows, with Aida and a group of her other slaves. The king and Amneris take their places on the throne.

Egyptian soldiers pass in review before the king. At the climax of the procession Radames enters.

The king greets his victorious general. Radames kneels. Amneris places the crown of victory on his head, and the king offers him anything he may wish for.

"First let the prisoners be brought forward," says Radames.

The prisoners are brought in. One of them is Amonasro.

"My father!" cries Aida.

She goes to him.

"Do not betray me," he warns her. He wears an officer's uniform. His captors have not recognized him as the king of Ethiopia.

He tells the Egyptian king that Amonasro was killed in battle, and he begs mercy for the prisoners. Aida, the other slaves, and the prisoners add their pleas to his.

Ramphis and the other priests demand death for the captives. But Radames' love for Aida has softened his heart toward the Ethiopians.

"You swore to grant my wish?" he asks the king. "Then set the prisoners free."

Ramphis protests. These prisoners are enemies. If they are pardoned, they will be free to attack again.

Radames replies that there is no danger of another Ethiopian uprising now that Amonasro is dead.

Ramphis proposes that Aida and her father be kept in Egypt as a pledge of peace, while the rest of the prisoners go free.

The king agrees to this, and, as a reward, he offers Radames the hand of Amneris in marriage.

Amneris is jubilant; Radames is dismayed.

Amonasro tells the despairing Aida, "Take heart. Happy events are in store for your country."

The scene of Act III is the bank of the Nile. It is night, with stars and a bright moon. Nearby is the temple of Isis.

Amneris, Ramphis, and their attendants alight from a boat. They have come to spend the night in prayer on the eve of Amneris' marriage to Radames.

The group disappears into the temple.

Aida enters. She has come to meet Radames. She dreads the thought of what he may say to her. If he bids her a last farewell, she has resolved to throw herself into the Nile. She thinks of her native land—the beautiful, beloved land she may never see again.

Amonasro appears. He has followed her so that they may talk in secret. Spies have told him that the Ethiopians are gathering for another attack.

"This time we shall win," he says. "I have only to know which path the enemy will take."

"But who can discover it?" says Aida.

"You can discover it," says her father. "Radames loves you. He leads the Egyptians. Do you understand?"

Aida refuses to betray Radames.

The hated Egyptians have spread terror and death throughout Ethiopia, says Amonasro. Now she will not lift a hand to save her country. He thrusts her away from him, saying she is not worthy to be his daughter.

She answers at last that she is still his daughter. She will do as he asks.

Radames approaches, and Amonasro hides among the palm trees.

Radames is overjoyed at seeing Aida.

But tomorrow, she says, he will be wedded to Amneris—for how can he hope to free himself from the love of the princess, the will of the king, and the wrath of the priests?

Radames tells her the Ethiopians have risen again and he will lead the Egyptians against them. When he returns, victorious and more famous than ever, he will confess his true feelings to the king. He believes the king will reward him. Aida will be his reward.

Aida protests that she is afraid of Amneris' vengeance. It is better, she says, that they run away.

Radames hesitates.

"You no longer love me!" says Aida. "Go—go to Amneris!"

"Never!" cries Radames. He has decided. He and Aida will escape to Ethiopia.

Which road shall they take, she asks, to avoid the Egyptian armies?

"The same path our troops will take when they attack the Ethiopians," he replies. "It will be deserted until tomorrow."

"Which path is that?" she asks.

"The Pass of Napata," he answers.

Amonasro comes from his hiding place. "The Pass of Napata!" he repeats. "My people shall be there!"

"Who has overheard us?" exclaims Radames.

"Aida's father and Ethiopia's king," answers Amonasro.

Aida asks Radames to trust in her. Amonasro promises him, "Aida's love will raise you to a throne."

Radames will not be consoled. His only thought is that he has betrayed his country.

"Come," says Amonasro. "Beyond the Nile trusted soldiers wait for us."

As he tries to draw Radames away, Amneris rushes from the temple where she has been listening. "Traitor!" she cries.

She is followed by Ramphis, other priests, and guards.

Amonasro drags his daughter away, as Radames surrenders to Ramphis.

Act IV begins in a hall in the king's palace. To the left is a gateway leading to the underground hall of judgment. To the right is a passageway to the prison where Radames awaits trial.

Amneris is crouching before the gate. She determines to make a last effort to save Radames and win him for herself. She orders the guards to bring him to her.

When he is brought into the hall, she tells him the priests are assembling to decide his fate. If he will defend himself, she will plead for him with all the power of her position.

He answers that all his hope and happiness are gone and he is ready to die. "You have taken Aida from me," he says. "Perhaps you have killed her."

"No," says Amneris. "Her father was killed, but Aida escaped."

Radames prays that she may find her way safely home.

"If I save you," says Amneris, "promise me you will never see her again."

Radames answers that he would rather die than give up his love for Aida.

In a frenzy, Amneris cries that he has turned her love to hate.

Priests appear on the way to the judgment hall. Guards lead Radames after them.

Amneris listens. She hears Ramphis ask Radames if he is guilty of treason. Radames refuses to speak.

His fate is decided. He shall be buried alive.

Amneris hears the sentence. She attacks the priests as they come up out of the judgment hall.

"Radames is a traitor," they tell her, "and he must die."

The final scene shows the temple of Vulcan, with a dark crypt beneath it. Radames has been lowered into the crypt. Above, two priests are hammering a stone in place to close the opening.

Someone moves in the darkness. Someone speaks. It is Aida. She has made her way into the tomb and hidden herself there so that they may die together.

They hear the chant of the priests and priestesses.

"Our hymn of death," says Aida.

Radames struggles to move the stone from the opening of the tomb so that her life may be saved, but it is too heavy for him to lift. They bid farewell to the earth and wait for death.

Amneris, dressed in mourning, throws herself upon the stone above and prays for the soul of Radames. Aida dies in Radames' arms.

# Faust

In 1839, when Charles Gounod was twenty-one and a student in the Paris Conservatory, he won the Prix de Rome for composition. The award gave him the privilege of studying in Rome, and for most of the next three years he was a student there. During this period he first thought of composing an opera based on Goethe's great dramatic poem, *Faust*.

Not until 1858, however, did he actually start work on the opera. By this time he had composed a good deal of music, including several operas which were not particularly successful. *Faust* was first performed in Paris on March 19, 1859. For a while it appeared that the new opera would be no more successful than the others, but it soon became popular throughout Europe.

The setting of the opera is Germany in the Middle Ages. The curtain rises on a gloomy study where Faust

169

sits alone. The old philosopher is weary of the world and his struggles to find the meaning of life.

Outside his window passers-by greet the Easter morning with a song. The happy voices seem to mock the old philosopher. He lifts a cup of poison he has prepared. Before he can drink, a chorus outside begins a song praising the beauty of the earth and ending, "Rejoice and pray."

"If I pray, who will hear me?" he asks himself, and in his bitterness, he calls upon Satan to come to his aid.

A stranger appears. He wears a velvet cloak, and he carries a sword. He has the appearance of a dashing young nobleman. He is Mephistopheles, the spirit of evil.

He asks what it is that Faust wishes. Is it gold, glory, a kingdom?

It is none of these, answers Faust. He wishes only to be young again.

Mephistopheles offers to grant his wish in exchange for Faust's soul.

The philosopher hesitates.

"See what I can show you," says Mephistopheles. He gestures, and a vision appears—a vision of a lovely girl at a spinning wheel.

With no more hesitation, Faust signs the pact with Mephistopheles. At once he is transformed into a young man.

Eagerly he asks when he will see the girl again.

"Today," answers Mephistopheles.

Act II takes place at a village fair. Valentine, a soldier, enters and is joined by his friend, Wagner. Valentine is going away to the wars, and he is anxious at leaving his young sister, Marguerite, alone and unprotected. Siebel, a village boy, promises to watch over her.

Valentine is reassured, although he is sad at the thought of leaving his friends and home.

As a cheering note, Wagner proposes that they all drink together. He begins a song. Mephistopheles enters and interrupts the song. He knows a better one, he says, and he sings "The Golden Calf," a cynical song praising the power of wealth.

He tells the fortunes of Wagner, Siebel, and Valentine and predicts misfortune for all three. He tastes the wine and declares it is not fit to drink.

"I'll see if I can find you something better," he says. He strikes the sign in front of the inn, and wine flows from it. Insolently he proposes a toast to Marguerite.

Angry at the stranger's insulting manner, Valentine challenges him to fight.

They draw swords. At a sign from Mephistopheles, Valentine's sword breaks in his hand.

Now the townspeople know that the power of evil is among them. The men turn the crosses of their swords toward Mephistopheles.

"While we bear this sign, you cannot harm us," they say, as they leave.

Mephistopheles has shrunk from them. Faust enters and asks what has happened.

"It was only talk," says Mephistopheles, recovering his self-possession. "How can I best serve you?"

Faust asks first to see the girl who appeared in the vision.

Mephistopheles promises that she shall soon be here, and while the villagers are dancing, the girl enters. She is Marguerite, Valentine's sister.

Faust speaks to the girl. He offers his arm and asks if he may walk with her.

She answers that she has no need of an arm to help her on her way. She leaves, and he gazes after her in fascination.

Mephistopheles asks him how he fared.

"Not well," answers Faust, and Mephistopheles promises to help him.

Village girls whisper to one another that Marguerite would not let the handsome young lord escort her home. Then the dance goes on.

The scene of Act III is the garden outside Marguerite's cottage. Siebel comes to pick a bouquet for her, but each time he picks a flower it withers in his hand. He recalls the fortune told him by Mephistopheles—that every flower he touches will die.

He goes to the shrine where Marguerite comes to pray. He dips his hand in the bowl of holy water. Again he picks a flower. This time it remains fresh.

"The power of Satan is gone!" he says, and he goes about the garden, gathering more flowers.

Mephistopheles and Faust enter. Siebel does not see them as he puts his bouquet down on the doorstep and goes away.

Mephistopheles looks contemptuously at the boy's offering. He tells Faust to wait while he fetches a rarer gift.

Alone in the garden, Faust looks worshipfully on Marguerite's cottage. Mephistopheles returns with a handsome jewel-casket which he sets outside the door. Then he and Faust leave the garden.

Marguerite comes out of the cottage. Sitting at her spinning wheel, she sings to herself. She is thinking of the man who spoke to her at the fair. She recalls his kind voice, his gentle manner.

Her thoughts turn to her brother. She prays that he may come safely home.

Seeing the bouquet, she tells herself that Siebel must have left it there.

She sees the casket and opens it. "Oh, heaven!" she cries, dazzled by the sight of the jewels it contains.

She decks herself out in the jewels. There is a mirror in the casket. She looks at herself in childlike delight and wishes that *he* could see her—the young man who spoke to her at the fair.

Martha, an old neighbor woman, comes bustling in and exclaims over the jewels.

"They are not mine," says Marguerite. "They were left here by mistake."

"No, they are yours," says Martha. She is sure they are the gift of some nobleman.

Mephistopheles returns. He tells Martha that her husband is dead and has sent his blessing.

"Has he sent nothing more?" asks the old woman.

"No," answers Mephistopheles. He advises her to find someone wealthier and more tender-hearted, and he leads her away. It is all a ruse to leave Faust and Marguerite alone together.

Faust has come back. Marguerite says modestly that she must go, but she lingers.

She takes a flower and recites to herself, "He loves me—he loves me not," as she picks off the petals. "He loves me," she finishes.

"The flower speaks truly," says Faust. "He loves you."

She confesses her love for him.

The hour is late, and she tells him she must go. She disappears into the house.

Believing he has gone, she opens her window and looks out into the night. "He loves me!" she repeats.

"Marguerite!" he cries. He rushes to her, as the watching Mephistopheles bursts into jeering, triumphant laughter.

Act IV finds Marguerite alone outside her house. Time has passed, and Faust has deserted her. Village girls laugh mockingly as they pass.

Siebel comes to her and swears that Faust shall be punished, but she will hear no ill of him. He loves her, she says, but his evil companion will not set him free.

She leaves for church.

Spirited music sounds in the distance. Soldiers are returning from the wars. As they march into sight, villagers are on hand to welcome them.

One of the soldiers is Valentine. He calls to Siebel and asks for Marguerite. The boy answers that he thinks she is in church.

The soldiers march away, followed by the crowd of villagers. Valentine stays with Siebel. The boy is ill at ease, and Valentine asks him what has happened.

"I cannot tell you," answers Siebel.

Valentine is alarmed. He starts toward the church.

Faust and Mephistopheles enter. Faust is remorseful over the unhappiness he has caused Marguerite. He has come back to her.

Mephistopheles sings a serenade to call the girl out of the house. Faust tries vainly to quiet him.

Valentine hears the serenade. Certain that it was intended as an insult to his sister, he challenges the two.

Faust crosses swords with Valentine. Mephistopheles guides Faust's sword, and Valentine falls.

Mephistopheles leads Faust away. Villagers arrive, and Marguerite enters.

She sees Valentine and calls his name. He turns away from her. "Your shame has destroyed me!" he cries, and as he dies, he curses her.

The next scene is a chapel adjoining the church. Marguerite is kneeling there in prayer. The voice of Mephistopheles forbids her to pray. Invisible demons call her name.

Mephistopheles rises out of a tomb and claims her soul as his own. She screams in terror. Worshippers coming from church find her lying in a faint.

The scene of Act V is a prison cell. Marguerite is sleeping on a bed of straw. In a fit of madness she has killed her new-born child. Now, convicted of the crime, she has been sentenced to death.

Faust and Mephistopheles come to rescue her—Faust because of his love for her, Mephistopheles because he is determined her soul shall be his.

The guard has been put to sleep. Mephistopheles has the keys to the prison. He waits outside, while Faust wakens Marguerite and tells her the way is clear for her escape. But they must hurry. It will soon be day, and daybreak is the time set for her execution.

Marguerite's mind wanders back to the time of their

first meeting. She fancies they are together again in her garden.

He begs her to come away. Mephistopheles returns to the cell and tells them the time is short.

She shrinks from him and begins to pray. Faust implores her to come with him, while Mephistopheles urges them to hurry.

Heaven has heard Marguerite's prayer. As she dies, a chorus of angels proclaims that she is saved. Defeated in his effort to gain her soul, Mephistopheles lays hold of Faust and sweeps him away to his doom.

# Carmen

The original *Carmen* was a story by the French author, Prosper Mérimée. His fellow countryman, Georges Bizet, composed an opera based on the story. The first performance—in Paris on March 3, 1875—was not a failure, but neither was it an outstanding success. Three months afterward Bizet died at the age of thirty-six, never to know that he had written one of the enduring masterpieces of opera.

The story is laid in Spain about 1820. The first scene shows a square in Seville. On the right is a tobacco factory. At the back is a bridge. On the left is a guardhouse.

Soldiers are lounging about the guardhouse. One of them is Morales, an officer.

Micaela, a village girl, comes hesitantly into the square. She tells Morales she is looking for a soldier named Don José.

"He is not here now," answers the officer, "but he will be when the guard changes."

Micaela goes away.

The relief guard appears, and among the soldiers are Lieutenant Zuniga and Don José. Street boys come marching in with the guard. They parade across the square, playing soldier and imitating the sound of trumpets.

After the guard has changed, Don José and Lieutenant Zuniga stand talking outside the guardhouse.

Zuniga looks at the tobacco factory and asks if that is where the girls go to make cigarettes.

"Yes," answers Don José, "and there are some lively ones among them."

"Are they pretty?" asks Zuniga.

Don José answers that he doesn't know—he has little interest in them.

The noon bell rings. The cigarette girls come out of the factory. Last of all comes Carmen, a bold-eyed gypsy girl. She is surrounded by the men who have been waiting. "We are your slaves," they tell her. "When will you be in love with us?"

"When shall I be in love?" says Carmen. "I don't know. Perhaps never—perhaps tomorrow."

Of all the men in the square, Don José alone has shown no interest in her. He sits apart, working on the chain he is making for his sword.

Carmen is piqued by his indifference. She throws him a flower. It strikes him, and he starts to his feet.

Laughing, she runs away. The factory bell rings again, calling the girls back to work. The crowd leaves. Don José is left alone.

The gypsy girl's boldness has astounded him. He picks up the flower and tucks it into his vest, as Micaela comes back to the square.

She tells him she has come from his mother, who has sent him a letter, some money, and a kiss.

She goes away while he reads the letter. His mother has written that she hopes he will marry Micaela.

"I shall obey you, mother," he says. "She shall be my wife."

There is a disturbance in the factory. Zuniga orders Don José to investigate. Don José goes into the factory and returns bringing Carmen.

There has been a fight. Carmen has wounded another girl.

Zuniga speaks to her. "What have you to say?"

Her only answer is an impudent little song.

"Very well," he says. "You can sing your song to the walls of the jail."

Soldiers place Carmen in a chair and tie her hands. Zuniga goes to write the order for her imprisonment. Don José is left to guard her.

She watches him. "You will do as I say, because you

love me," she says. "The flower I gave you was enchanted, and it has done its work!"

He tells her not to speak.

She begins to sing of her friend, Lillas Pastia, who has a tavern near the ramparts of the city where she will go with her new love.

Again he commands her not to speak.

"I did not speak to you," she says. "I was only singing a song to myself." She adds that she is thinking, too—surely that can do him no harm. She is thinking of a soldier who loves her and knows well that she might love him in return.

"Carmen!" he exclaims. "If I love you, will you promise to love me, too?"

"Yes," she answers.

He loosens the rope on her hands.

Zuniga comes with the order for Don José to take Carmen to prison.

People crowd the square as the girl is led away. She and Don José have agreed on a plan of action. She pushes him and he falls. She throws off the rope and escapes over the bridge.

The second act takes place two months later. The scene is Lillas Pastia's tavern. Carmen is there with two other gypsy girls, Frasquita and Mercédès. Morales and Zuniga are also there. Zuniga bears Carmen no ill will because of her escape, but she is cool toward him.

Lillas Pastia sends word that it is time to close the tavern. The officers prepare to leave, and Zuniga asks Carmen to go with him. She ignores him.

A torchlight procession comes down the road. A crowd is honoring the toreador, Escamillo, hero of the bull-fights at Granada.

Zuniga invites them in. The toreador and his friends accept the invitation. As they all drink together, Escamillo tells of the excitement and danger of the bull ring.

Carmen is at his side, pouring him wine. He grows more and more attentive to her.

He and his friends go their way. The officers follow them.

Carmen and the two other gypsy girls stay behind after the tavern is closed. Two smugglers, Dancairo and Remendado, come forward. They need the girls' help in a new venture. To succeed, say the men, they must all travel together.

Frasquita and Mercédès are willing to go, but Carmen says she must wait for Don José, who has been sent to prison for allowing her to escape.

"Are you sure he will come?" asks Dancairo.

"Listen!" says Carmen. "He is already here."

They hear him singing outside the tavern.

The others leave Carmen alone for her reunion with Don José. It is a tender meeting, but almost at once he is angry and jealous when he learns that she has been dancing for the soldiers. To pacify him, she sings and dances for him alone.

He stops her. In the distance he has heard a bugle blowing retreat. It is the signal for all soldiers to return to quarters.

She is annoyed when he tells her he must go. She thought he loved her, she says, but the moment a bugle blows, he must be off. She throws his cap and sword at him. "Go back to the barracks!" she tells him.

He tries to convince her of his love. He shows her the flower she gave him. All through his days and nights in prison he kept it in memory of her.

If he really loved her, she says, he would take her away into the mountains where they could be free.

Don José protests. He is a soldier, and that would mean deserting the army. "It must not be," he says.

"Then good-by forever," she says.

Sadly he turns toward the door.

There is a knocking outside. Lieutenant Zuniga bursts into the tavern. Insultingly he orders Don José to go about his business. They quarrel. Zuniga strikes him, and Don José draws his sword.

The gypsies and the two smugglers rush in. They overpower Zuniga.

Don José has resisted an officer. If he stays he will be sent back to prison.

"Now will you join us?" asks Carmen.

He answers that he has no choice.

The scene of Act III is the smugglers' camp in the mountains. The smugglers are waiting in the darkness of night for a chance to slip past the coast guard with their contraband goods.

Dancairo and Remendado leave to see whether or not the way is clear. Some of the others gather by the fire. Don José stands apart, looking down over the rocks.

Carmen asks him what he sees down there.

He answers that he is thinking of a woman who lives in the world below—his mother, who believes he is an honest man.

Carmen has begun to grow weary of him. She tells him he had better go to his mother.

He threatens her life if she ever again hints at separation.

She goes to the fire where Frasquita and Mercédès are telling their fortunes with cards. Carmen tells her own fortune. She sees only death in the cards.

Dancairo and Remendado return to report the road is clear. The smugglers leave, Don José last of all. He has been detailed to stay and guard the camp.

Micaela enters. Word has reached her that Don José is with the smugglers, and she has come to find him.

She sees him standing guard. He catches sight of her and fires a shot at her, thinking she is a spy. In terror she drops out of sight behind the rocks.

A moment later Escamillo enters, with Don José behind him.

The toreador ruefully complains that he almost got in the way of the shot. Don José welcomes him and asks if he means to stay.

Escamillo answers that he has come here only to find the girl he loves. "She is a charming gypsy," he says. "She once loved a soldier who deserted the army, but I hear she is weary of him."

Angered, Don José challenges him to a fight. Escamillo realizes his mistake. He draws his knife and prepares to defend himself.

Carmen returns with the rest of the band. She separates the fighters.

Dancairo asks the toreador to leave. Escamillo stays long enough to invite them all to the bullfights in Seville. "Whoever loves me will come," he says, looking at Carmen.

Don José lunges at him and the smugglers hold him back, as Escamillo strolls away.

Don José says tensely, "I warn you, Carmen, not to torture me!"

She only shrugs.

Remendado spies someone hiding among the rocks. He goes out and returns with the frightened Micaela.

She begs Don José to come home.

He had better go, says Carmen. He refuses to leave

her. Only when Micaela tells him his mother is dying does he agree to go. But it is only for the present, he says to Carmen. He has no thought of leaving her for good.

Act IV takes place in Seville on the day of the bullfights. The curtain rises on the square outside the arena. Zuniga is there, talking with Frasquita and Mercédès. Escamillo enters with Carmen, who is radiantly happy.

Frasquita and Mercédès draw her aside. She is in danger, they say. Don José has been seen in the square.

Carmen is not afraid. "If he wants to speak to me, I am here."

The crowd goes into the amphitheater. Don José appears. He is haggard and unkempt. Carmen waits for him. They are alone together.

Desperately he begs her to come with him.

"No," she says. "I was born free, and I shall die free." She starts toward the arena.

Don José accuses her of preferring the toreador to him.

She readily admits it. Once more she starts toward the amphitheater where Escamillo is being acclaimed a hero. Don José bars her way. He draws a knife and stabs her. She falls and dies.

He kneels beside her. The crowd comes out of the arena. Escamillo appears on the steps.

"Take me prisoner. I have killed her," cries Don José, and he sobs, "Ah, Carmen, my adored one!"

# Manon

*Manon Lescaut,* by the Abbé Prévost, was a popular French novel of the eighteenth century. In 1883 the French composer Jules Massenet finished the score of an opera based on the story.

*Manon* was first performed in Paris on January 19, 1884. It was an immediate success.

The time of the opera is 1721. Act I takes place outside an inn at Amiens. Three actresses, Poussette, Javotte, and Rosette, come into the courtyard. With them are two men—Guillot, minister of finance, and Bretigny, a nobleman. All are guests at the inn, and they shout for something to eat and drink until waiters come out and serve them in the summer house.

The coach arrives from a neighboring village. One of the passengers is Manon, a girl of sixteen. This is her first trip away from home, and she is breathlessly excited.

189

Her cousin, Lescaut, a swaggering guardsman, is there to meet her. He goes to find her luggage.

Guillot and Bretigny see the girl standing alone. Both are charmed by her loveliness. Guillot boldly approaches her and tells her he is very wealthy.

To Manon he is only a ridiculous old man. She cannot help laughing at him. Her cousin comes back, and Guillot hurries off in confusion.

Two fellow guardsmen have been waiting for Lescaut to join them in a game of cards. He leaves with them, after telling Manon to wait there and warning her to pay no attention to any foolish men who may speak to her.

She sees the three actresses in the summer house. How beautiful they are, she thinks, and how happy they must be! But she can never hope for such a life. She is on her way to a convent, where she must put all worldly pleasures behind her.

A young nobleman enters—the Chevalier Des Grieux. A seat has been reserved for him on the next coach, which will take him to the home of his father.

He sees Manon. She has already seen him. At once they are attracted to each other. He speaks to her.

She tells him about herself. She is only a poor girl, she says, not wicked, but often accused of loving pleasure too much. "Now," she says, "I am on my way to a convent. This is all the story of Manon Lescaut."

He will not believe in such a fate. Once the convent

gates close behind her, she will be lost to him forever.

A carriage arrives. It belongs to Guillot. He has sent it for Manon, in the hope that she will agree to meet him.

It almost seems that fate is pointing the way for Manon and Des Grieux. They take Guillot's carriage. They drive away in it toward Paris.

Lescaut returns and searches for his cousin. He sees Guillot and accuses him of having made off with her. The innkeeper informs them that Manon is gone—she and a handsome young man have driven off in Guillot's carriage.

The scene of Act II is an apartment in Paris. Des Grieux is writing at a desk. Manon leans over his shoulder and together they read what he has written. It is a letter to the count, Des Grieux' father. The young man is asking permission to marry Manon.

A maid brings word that two men are outside. One is Manon's cousin, Lescaut. "The other," she tells Manon in a low voice, "is someone who is in love with you— Bretigny, the man who lives near here."

The two men enter. Lescaut demands to know whether or not Des Grieux intends to marry Manon. Des Grieux answers that he does, indeed. As proof, he shows the letter he has just written his father.

Bretigny manages to speak to Manon alone. Tonight, he tells her, young Des Grieux is going to be kidnapped by order of the Count Des Grieux. The count does not approve of Manon, and by separating her and his son, he hopes to end the affair.

Manon says she must warn Des Grieux.

"If you do, it will mean misery for you both," says Bretigny. "If you do not, good fortune waits for you."

Lescaut leaves. Bretigny leaves with him. Des Grieux goes out to mail his letter.

Manon's thoughts are confused. She is torn between her love for Des Grieux and her doubts for their future. Perhaps it is true that she would bring him only misfortune.

She sees the little table where their evening meal is spread. She recalls the times when it was their happy meeting place. Sadly she bids it farewell.

Des Grieux returns. He tells her of his dream of their future—of a small house in the country where they can be together always.

There is a knock at the door. She tries to tell him of the plot to separate them, but she is too late. He has already gone to the door. There are sounds of a struggle. He does not come back.

"My poor chevalier!" she cries, and she runs to the window in time to see the carriage that is taking him away.

The time of Act III is months later. The first scene is a festival in Paris. Manon has come there with Bretigny.

Guillot has brought Poussette, Javotte, and Rosette,

but they have run away from him. Now he has plans for taking Manon away from Bretigny.

Manon appears, surrounded by admirers. But she is weary of admiration. Leaving Bretigny, she wanders off into the crowd.

Count Des Grieux enters. He has come to Paris to visit his son. The young man is at the Seminary of St. Sulpice, preparing to enter the holy orders. This he tells Bretigny, as they talk together.

Manon overhears part of the conversation. She sends Bretigny away so that she may speak with the count alone.

"I think you were talking of the man who was once in love with a girl I knew," she says. "I want to know if he has forgotten his old love."

The count knows he is speaking with Manon. It is wiser not to dwell on the past, he tells her.

She persists. Does Des Grieux still suffer? Does he blame the girl who turned so quickly to a new love affair?

The count answers that with the help of God the young man has learned to forget, and he takes leave of her.

Bretigny returns, along with Guillot. Guillot has carried out the plan by which he hopes to win Manon away from Bretigny. He has brought the entire ballet of the opera here to perform for her.

Manon cares little for the performance. She can think

only of Des Grieux. "He cannot have forgotten me," she tells herself, and, turning away from the festival, she orders a carriage to St. Sulpice.

The next scene is the reception room at St. Sulpice Seminary. Women are praising young Des Grieux, as they leave the chapel. "How eloquently he spoke! How fine and clear his language!"

Count Des Grieux comes into the reception room. His son joins him.

The count compliments him on his success, but asks if he really wishes to bind himself to the church.

"Yes," answers the young man firmly. "I feel only bitterness and disgust for the world."

The count goes away. The young man goes back to the chapel.

Manon enters. She sends a porter to find Des Grieux and bring him to her. The young man returns and starts back at the sight of her.

"What are you doing here?" he cries. "Go away!"

She asks him to remember that they were once in love.

"Our love was meant to die," he says. "You were faithless—you are gone from my memory and my heart."

She begs to be forgiven. Again he orders her to leave him, and she refuses. He can pretend no longer. He confesses his love for her.

The scene of Act IV is the gaming room of a fashionable Paris hotel. Manon's cousin, Lescaut, is there. The three actresses are there, along with Guillot. Guillot is angry when he sees Manon enter with Des Grieux.

He challenges the young man to a game of cards.

They play. Time after time Guillot loses. At last he accuses Des Grieux of cheating.

At once the place is in an uproar. The police arrive. Guillot demands Des Grieux' arrest, and Manon is arrested as his accomplice.

Because of his father's influence, Des Grieux is soon released. Guillot's revenge on Manon is more successful. She is tried and sentenced to be deported.

At the beginning of Act V, Des Grieux is waiting by the road to Havre. It is the road over which Manon will soon pass with other prisoners who are being sent to the penal colony in Louisiana.

Lescaut arrives and bribes a guard to let the girl go free.

The prisoners pass along the road. Manon is with them. She sees Des Grieux and forgets how exhausted and ill she is.

He promises to take her away where they can be happy together.

"Yes, I can still be happy," she says, as if in a dream. "Let us talk of the past—of the inn and the carriage and our little table and your black robe at St. Sulpice . . ."

Then, realizing she is dying, she murmurs her last words, "This is all the story of Manon Lescaut."

# Cavalleria Rusticana

*Cavalleria Rusticana* ("Rustic Chivalry") is an opera in one act. It is based on a story by Giovanni Verga, an Italian writer of the late nineteenth century. The young Italian composer Pietro Mascagni heard of an opera contest conducted by a publisher in Milan. Working at furious speed, he wrote the score of *Cavalleria Rusticana*. He entered it in the contest and won first prize.

The opera was first performed in Rome on May 17, 1890. It won overnight fame for the composer.

The time of the opera is the nineteenth century. The place is a village in Sicily.

Before the curtain rises, Turiddu, a young villager, sings a serenade. His song is in praise of Lola "with lips like crimson berries." He swears that if he found himself in heaven, he would be filled with grief if she were not there, too.

197

The curtain rises on the public square. At one side is the church, at the other is the inn kept by Mamma Lucia. It is Easter Sunday, and people cross the square on their way to church.

Santuzza, a village girl, comes to the inn and asks for Turiddu.

Mamma Lucia tells her, "My son is not here. He has gone to Francofonte to buy wine."

"No!" says Santuzza. "Last night he was seen here in the village."

If that is true, replies Mamma Lucia, she knows nothing of it.

Alfio, the teamster, comes into the square accompanied by a crowd of his friends. He asks Mamma Lucia for some of the good old wine he is used to buying at the inn.

"Turiddu has gone to Francofonte to fetch some," she answers.

"No, he is here," says Alfio. "I saw him this morning not far from my house."

"What!" exclaims Mamma Lucia in surprise, and Santuzza whispers, "Be quiet!"

Alfio leaves. When they are alone, Mamma Lucia asks the girl, "Why did you bid me be quiet?"

Santuzza reminds her that Turiddu was once promised to Lola, another village girl. Then he went away to war, and when he came home he found Lola married to Alfio.

"So he turned to me, and I loved him," says Santuzza, "but Lola was jealous of our happiness. She took him from me. Now I am dishonored and alone, and Turiddu and Lola are in love again."

That was why she silenced Mamma Lucia—to keep her from saying something that might arouse Alfio's suspicions.

Mamma Lucia is shocked and saddened.

"Pray for me," begs Santuzza, "and I shall see Turiddu and plead with him to be faithful to me."

Mamma Lucia goes into the church.

Turiddu enters and tells Santuzza he has just come back from Francofonte.

"It is not true," she says. "This morning you were seen near Lola's house."

He accuses her of spying on him. He will not be a slave to her jealousy, he declares.

They are interrupted by the voice of Lola. She is singing as she comes into the square.

She knows Santuzza has been cast out of the church because of her sins, but she asks the girl maliciously, "Are you not going to church?"

Santuzza retorts that none ought to go except those who have not sinned.

Lola answers mockingly, "May the Lord bless you," and goes on into the church. Turiddu turns to follow her.

"Stay with me!" says Santuzza.

"Why do you follow me? Why do you spy on me!" he cries. He throws her to the ground and rushes off.

At the height of Santuzza's rage and despair, Alfio enters.

"Lola has gone with Turiddu!" she says.

He asks in surprise, "What do you mean?"

"When your work takes you away from home," she says, "Lola and Turiddu are together!"

He threatens her with death if she is lying.

She swears she has told the truth. He believes her at last.

But already she regrets her outburst. "It is shameful of me to have spoken so," she says.

"No, *they* are shameful," says Alfio, "and before this day is over, I'll have revenge."

He leaves. Santuzza follows him, and for a while the square is deserted. Then the worshippers leave the church, and Mamma Lucia goes into the inn.

Lola and Turiddu come out of the church together. She says she must go home to Alfio, but he persuades her to stay. He calls to his friends and asks them to drink with him. While they are drinking, Alfio comes up to the inn.

Turiddu offers him a drink.

Alfio's answer is a deliberate insult. "If I drink with you, I might be drinking poison," he says.

Lola is frightened. Fearing trouble, the other women lead her away.

In the Sicilian manner the two men challenge each other. They embrace, and Turiddu viciously bites Alfio's ear.

"We understand each other," says Alfio, and he goes away to wait for Turiddu.

Turiddu calls his mother. She comes out of the inn, and he tells her he is going for a walk. "Before I go," he says, "give me your blessing as you did on the morning I went away to war. And if I do not come back, take care of Santuzza and be a mother to her."

"Why do you speak so strangely?" she asks.

He pretends the wine has gone to his head. "God forgive me!" he cries and hurries away toward the place where the duel is to be fought.

Santuzza enters. She and Turiddu's mother cling together. People pour into the square. Their voices rise in an excited murmur.

A woman rushes into the square, crying out, "They've killed our friend, Turiddu!"

Santuzza falls to the ground. Mamma Lucia faints in the arms of the women near her. Terror sweeps over the crowd, as the curtain falls.

# I Pagliacci

The Italian composer Ruggiero Leoncavallo wrote both the libretto and the musical score of *I Pagliacci*. *Pagliacci* is an Italian name for strolling actors. Leoncavallo based his story on a true incident in the lives of such a troupe.

The opera had its first performance in Milan on May 21, 1892. It was immediately successful.

*I Pagliacci* is introduced by Tonio, the clown. He steps before the curtain and tells the audience that the play they are about to see has been taken from life. Beneath their costumes, he says, actors are only human beings, feeling love and hate and loneliness like anyone else.

"With this thought," he says, "watch our play unfold."

The story is laid in southern Italy in the nineteenth century. The scene is a crossroads just outside a village, where a traveling theater has been set up. Tonio has come ahead and is waiting for the rest of the troupe.

Villagers enter. It is the day of the Feast of the Assumption, and they are dressed in their holiday best. They stare at the ugly, misshapen Tonio. Annoyed, he lies down in front of the theater and tries to ignore them.

"Here they are! Stand back!" shouts the crowd, and the rest of the *pagliacci* arrive. Beppe, who plays young men's roles, is leading a donkey hitched to a painted cart. In the cart are Canio and his wife, Nedda.

Canio is beating a bass drum, and when he has attracted the villagers' attention, he tells them about the performance to be given that evening.

Tonio goes hobbling to help Nedda out of the cart. Canio gives him a box on the ear and lifts her out himself.

The crowd laughs at Tonio, who mutters angrily and disappears back of the theater.

Beppe has led the donkey off. When he returns, Canio and some of the villagers are about to leave for a nearby tavern.

"Wait for me," says Beppe. He throws down his whip and runs into the theater to change his clothes.

Canio calls to Tonio, "Are you coming?"

"I'm rubbing down the donkey," the clown calls back. "Go on ahead of me."

One of the villagers says jokingly to Canio, "Be careful. He is only staying behind so he can be alone with Nedda."

The joke does not amuse Canio. "Such a game had better not be played on me," he says. "The stage is not the same as life. When I play the part of Pagliaccio and find my lady with someone else, it is only a scene for the pleasure of the crowd. But if my wife should really deceive me, it would be a far different story!"

Bagpipers approach on the way to the church service. Canio leaves, after reminding the crowd, "Don't forget. This evening at seven."

The pipers come down the road, and the villagers follow them off to church.

Nedda is uneasy after Canio's fit of jealousy. But the sun is bright. It is a fine summer day. Before long she is singing a lighthearted song to the birds.

When she finishes, she discovers she is not alone. Tonio is there.

"I thought you had gone!" she says sharply.

He could not go, he says, because her singing held him fascinated.

She laughs at him.

"I know I am ugly," he says, "yet I have a heart, and I love you."

She laughs again.

He makes a move toward her. She picks up Beppe's whip and strikes him with it.

"You'll pay for this!" he says furiously, as he leaves.

Tonio is hardly out of sight, when a young man appears. He is Nedda's lover, Silvio.

She is startled. "It is not wise for you to come here in the daytime," she tells him.

He answers that there is no risk. Canio and Beppe are at the tavern.

"But you almost met Tonio," she says.

"Ah, Tonio, the fool!" says Silvio, laughing.

"He is a fool, yet he may be dangerous," she says. "Just now I had to strike him with the whip."

"You must not go on living this way," he says. He asks her to come away with him.

Neither he nor Nedda sees that Tonio has stolen back. He stays long enough to spy on the lovers. Then he hurries off and returns, bringing Canio.

Silvio has persuaded Nedda to elope with him.

"Tonight at midnight I'll be waiting," he says.

"Till tonight," answers Nedda, "and I'll be yours forever."

Canio overhears the words. He dashes off after Silvio, while Tonio taunts Nedda, enjoying his revenge.

Canio returns. He was not able to catch the man or even see his face.

"But no matter," he says to Nedda, "because you will tell me his name."

She refuses.

"Who was it?" he shouts. "Tell me, and be quick!"

"No," she answers. "I'll never tell."

He draws a knife. Beppe appears, struggles with Canio, and takes the knife from him.

"Master, for the love of heaven!" cries Beppe, "the people are out of church and on their way to our play. You must calm yourself."

He takes Nedda into the theater.

The clown tells Canio, "Keep calm and wait. The fellow will come back—perhaps to see the play tonight."

Canio stands alone in front of the theater. He wonders how he can force himself to go on in the play when he is on the verge of madness. "But you are an actor," he tells himself. "Put on your costume and your make-up. The people pay you to amuse them, so you must go out on the stage and play your part while your heart is breaking!"

As the second scene begins, people are arriving for the performance. Silvio enters and takes a front seat.

Nedda comes out with a plate in which she collects money from the audience. She whispers to Silvio, "Be careful!"

The crowd grows quiet. The performance begins.

The play is the old story of Columbine. Columbine's husband, Pagliaccio, is not expected home until late, and she has invited her lover, Harlequin, to dinner. She has sent a boy, Taddeo, out for food.

Harlequin serenades her outside the window. Taddeo arrives with the basket of food and in ridiculous fashion tries to make love to her. Harlequin comes in through the window, kicks Taddeo, and drives him out. Harlequin and Columbine plot to give Pagliaccio a sleeping potion that night and run away together. While they are at dinner Taddeo comes to tell them Pagliaccio has returned.

Harlequin leaps out the window, and Columbine calls after him, "Till tonight—and I'll be yours forever," just as Pagliaccio enters.

The roles of Columbine and Pagliaccio are played by Nedda and Canio. Beppe plays Harlequin, and Tonio is in the role of Taddeo.

The play goes smoothly until Pagliaccio's entrance. Canio forgets his role. Once more he demands the name of Nedda's lover.

She tries to bring his mind back to the play.

"So you defy me!" shouts Canio. "Who was it? Tell me his name!"

The people in the audience are moved by what they think is an unusually lifelike performance.

"I'll never tell you his name," replies Nedda defiantly. "Not even if you kill me!"

She runs toward the audience. Canio catches her and stabs her.

Silvio leaps to his feet. Nedda, dying, calls to him.

"Ah, so it was you!" says Canio, and he drives his knife into Silvio's heart. Then, facing the audience, he cries out brokenly, "The comedy is ended!"

# La Bohème

The story of *La Bohème* was taken from the French novel, *Scenes of Bohemian Life,* by Henri Murger. It tells of the struggling young artists—the "Bohemians"— of Paris.

The novel must have reminded Giacomo Puccini of his own lean years before he became a successful composer. From 1880 to 1883 he was a student at the Conservatory of Milan. During this time and for years afterward he struggled against poverty and failure, but by 1895, when he began work on *La Bohème,* he had met with considerable success.

The opera had its world premiere in Turin, Italy, on February 1, 1896. At first it was coolly received. Critics found it frivolous and not worthy of the composer's talents. Before the end of the year, however, the new opera was on its way to success.

*La Bohème* takes place in Paris about 1830. The scene of Act I is the attic studio of four friends, Rodolfo, Marcello, Schaunard, and Colline. Rodolfo is a poet, Marcello a painter, Schaunard a musician, and Colline a philosopher.

It is Christmas Eve. Marcello and Rodolfo are alone. The painter is hard at work on a picture of the Red Sea. Every now and then he stops and blows on his fingers to warm them. The poet is at the window gazing out over the snow-covered roofs.

Marcello suggests they break up a chair for firewood. Rodolfo has another idea. He takes up a play he has written and they begin to burn it in the fireplace.

While they are enjoying the warmth, Colline enters and throws some books down upon the table. He has gone out to pawn them and found all the pawnshops closed on Christmas Eve.

He joins his friends at the fireplace. As long as the fire burns, he and Marcello praise Rodolfo's play. But when the last act is burned and the fire dies, they shout, "Down with the author!"

Two boys come in, delivering fuel, food, wine, and cigars. As they leave, Schaunard enters. It is he who has provided these luxuries. He has given some music lessons to an English lord, who paid him handsomely.

Rodolfo spreads a newspaper for a tablecloth. He and Marcello and Colline prepare to dine. Schaunard stops them. The food can be saved till later, he says. Christmas Eve is no time for dining at home.

There is a knock at the door. Benoit, the landlord, has come for the rent.

The four friends invite the old man in and greet him cordially. They give him wine, and when he is reeling from the effects of it, they push him out the door.

Schaunard divides his money among his friends and they make ready to go out into the Latin Quarter. Rodolfo decides to stay behind for a little while to finish an article he is writing, and his friends leave.

He finds he is not in the mood to write. As he throws down his pen, someone knocks timidly.

It is Mimi, a girl who lives in the building. She was on the stairs when her candle went out. She asks if he will light it for her.

She coughs, and he notices how pale she is.

"Are you ill?" he asks.

She answers that she is out of breath from climbing the stairs. Suddenly she grows faint. Her candle and key fall to the floor. Rodolfo helps her to a chair.

She recovers. He pours her some wine, and she drinks a little. All the time he is thinking how lovely she is.

He lights her candle. They bid each other good evening, and she goes out.

Almost at once she is back. "My key!" she says. "Where did I leave it?"

She is standing in the open doorway. A draft of air blows out her candle. Before he can light it again, his own candle blows out.

In the darkness she gropes her way to the table and puts her candle down. He closes the door. Together they feel about the floor, searching for her key. He finds it and slips it into his pocket. Their hands touch, and she draws away.

He tells her there is no use trying to find the key in the dark. He would rather they talked instead.

"May I tell you who I am?" he asks. He is a poet, he says, poor in worldly goods but rich in dreams. "Now will you tell me who you are?"

"They call me Mimi," she answers. She is a seamstress. Her work is embroidering flowers on cloth. She lives alone, and she does not often go to church, although she prays a great deal.

Rodolfo's friends shout from below. They are waiting for him.

He opens the window, and moonlight floods the room. He calls down to say that he is not alone. "Go to Momus and save us a place," he says.

He turns and sees Mimi standing in the moonlight. He gazes in rapture. "Say you love me," he says.

"I love you," she answers.

They leave together, Mimi clinging to his arm.

Act II takes place outside the Café Momus. People

are milling about. The café is so crowded that some of the tables have been moved outside. Marcello, Colline, and Schaunard take one of the outdoor tables. Rodolfo and Mimi come out of a shop where he has just bought a rose for her bonnet.

A vendor comes in pushing a little cart filled with Christmas toys and trinkets. Children gather around him and follow him when he leaves.

Mimi and the four friends are drinking toasts, when an elegantly dressed young woman enters, followed by a pompous-looking old man. Marcello turns pale. She is Musetta, who was once his sweetheart.

She chooses a table in sight of him. The old man, Alcindoro, objects to dining outside in the cold, but she orders him to sit down.

Marcello ignores her. Musetta tries to attract his attention. She talks loudly. She complains of the food and smashes a plate on the sidewalk.

At last she turns directly toward Marcello and begins to talk of what a beautiful and charming person she really is and how she knows perfectly well that he has not forgotten her.

When she sees that Marcello is no longer able to resist her charms, she plots to get rid of the old man.

She screams and says her shoe is pinching her foot. Alcindoro takes off her shoe, and she sends him away to buy another pair.

He is hardly out of sight before she is in Marcello's arms.

A waiter presents the bill. The four friends search their pockets and are surprised to find their money is gone. Musetta leaves the bill for Alcindoro to pay.

Soldiers march past and crowds go trailing after them. Musetta cannot walk in only one shoe, and Marcello and Colline carry her on their shoulders. The people cheer her, and she grandly acknowledges their applause. Mimi, Rodolfo, and Schaunard leave with the others.

Alcindoro returns carrying a pair of shoes. As he looks about for Musetta, a waiter hands him a bill. Staggered by the amount, the old man collapses into a chair.

The third act takes place at a tollgate near the Latin Quarter. To one side is a tavern with a signboard outside. The signboard is Marcello's painting of the Red Sea, now titled "The Port of Marseilles."

It is a cold morning, more than a month after the Christmas Eve party. Soldiers, guards, and streetsweepers are moving about. Musetta's voice comes from within the tavern.

Mimi enters. She is pale and ill, and a fit of coughing seizes her. She has come to find Marcello, who works at the tavern.

He comes out and invites her inside.

"Is Rodolfo there?" she asks.

"Yes," he answers.

"Then I cannot go inside," she says. She and Rodolfo have quarreled. As much in love as they are, they seem to bring each other only unhappiness. He is jealous and flies into rages. Now they have parted.

"Help us," she says. "We cannot help ourselves."

Rodolfo comes out of the tavern, and she hides behind a tree. He tells Marcello of his latest quarrel with Mimi.

The real reason for their quarrels, says Rodolfo, is that he is anxious and afraid. Mimi is ill, and he is so poor he can do nothing for her. He cannot even keep her from hunger and cold, and his love is not enough to make her well again.

Mimi overhears. "Ah, my life!" she cries. "It is ended!"

She begins to cough, and Rodolfo discovers her. He takes her in his arms.

Marcello hears Musetta's laughter. "With whom is she laughing!" he exclaims, and he stalks angrily into the tavern.

Mimi bids Rodolfo good-by. It is a tender and sad farewell, interrupted by the voices of Musetta and Marcello, who are quarreling fiercely.

The attic studio is the scene of Act IV. Rodolfo is sitting at the table with pen in hand. Marcello is at his easel. But they only pretend to work. Rodolfo thinks of Mimi. Marcello sees Musetta's face.

Schaunard and Colline come in bringing bread and a salted herring.

The four gather around the table and pretend they are enjoying a banquet complete with champagne. They decide that dancing would be appropriate after dinner, and they begin a quadrille. Colline and Schaunard engage in a mock quarrel. They fight a duel with the poker and fire tongs.

Suddenly Musetta appears. Mimi is here, she says. She is outside, exhausted from climbing the stairs.

Rodolfo and Marcello carry Mimi into the room and put her down on the bed.

She asks Rodolfo faintly if he wants her to be here with him.

"Always, always!" he answers.

Musetta tells the other friends softly that she found the girl on the street just now. Mimi felt as if she were dying, and she wished to see Rodolfo once more.

Musetta asks if there is coffee or wine in the house.

"Nothing," answers Marcello bitterly.

Now Mimi recognizes the others in the room. She smiles and speaks to them. She tells Marcello how good and kind Musetta is.

"I know," says Marcello, and he takes Musetta's hand.

Musetta gives him her earrings. "Go sell them," she says. "Bring back a doctor." Then she asks him to wait— she will go with him to bring a muff to warm Mimi's hands.

They leave together. Colline takes off his old coat, bids

it an affectionate farewell, and goes out to pawn it. Schaunard goes with him so that Rodolfo and Mimi may be alone for a while.

"My beautiful Mimi!" he says.

"Am I still beautiful?" she asks.

"As beautiful as a sunrise," he says.

"No—as a sunset," she says.

He gives her the little bonnet she left behind when they parted. She is happy that he has kept it.

Schaunard returns. Musetta comes bringing a muff, and Marcello brings medicine.

"The doctor will be here soon," he says.

Mimi puts her hands into the muff. She is delighted with its softness and warmth. Her eyes close. She murmurs in drowsy contentment.

Musetta heats the medicine over a spirit lamp. Schaunard has gone near the bed, and he tells Marcello quietly, "She is dead."

Colline returns with the money he has been paid for his coat. "Take this," he says to Musetta, and he goes to help Rodolfo, who is covering the window so that the sun will not shine on Mimi's face.

As Rodolfo turns, he sees the strange expressions of Marcello and Schaunard. "Mimi—Mimi!" he cries. In an agony of grief, he falls sobbing upon the bed.

# Tosca

Sardou's popular play *Tosca* had long interested Puccini as the subject for an opera. But Sardou was one of the giants of the French theater, and he was doubtful about entrusting his play to a man whom he considered no more than a promising young composer.

Puccini went to Paris for an interview with the playwright. Sardou asked him for a sample of the music he intended to write. Puccini had planned none of the music for *Tosca*, but he went to the piano and played parts of *La Bohème* and his earlier operas. Sardou was pleased with what he heard, and he signed a contract with the composer.

Puccini's *Tosca* was first performed in Rome on January 14, 1900.

The time of the opera is 1800. The first scene shows the inside of the church of Sant' Andrea della Valle in

Rome. At the right is the gate to the Attavani chapel. At the left is an artist's easel which holds a large canvas covered with a cloth. About the easel are paints, brushes, and a lunch basket.

A man staggers into the church. He is in ragged prison clothes. He goes to the Madonna and searches feverishly at the foot of the statue until he finds a key.

With the key he unlocks the gate and disappears into the Attavani chapel.

The old sacristan comes into the church, carrying a bundle of paint brushes. He grumbles that he has more cleaning than ever now that an artist is working there.

He peers into the basket to see what the artist has brought for lunch. The angelus sounds, and he kneels to pray. As the prayer ends, the artist, Mario Cavaradossi, enters. He uncovers the canvas, revealing a painting of a golden-haired Mary Magdalen.

The sacristan stares at it. The face is that of a lady who comes to the church every day to pray.

Cavaradossi admits he has been watching the lady and painting her features without her knowing.

He paints for a while, then stops to look at a miniature which he carries with him. The woman in his painting is blonde. The face in the miniature is dark. Both are beautiful, but while he paints the golden-haired lady, he is thinking only of the dark-eyed beauty, his beloved Tosca.

The sacristan asks Cavaradossi about the food in the basket—"Aren't you eating?"

"I am not hungry," answers the artist.

The sacristan looks greedily into the basket. He picks it up, sets it aside, and goes out.

The church is quiet. The man hiding in the chapel believes himself alone. He unlocks the gate.

The artist turns toward the man, who pauses in terror. Then the man recognizes the artist as a friend. He exclaims in relief, "Cavaradossi!"

"Angelotti!" cries the artist. He closes the side door of the church.

Once Angelotti was consul of the Roman republic. When the republic was overthrown, he was imprisoned in the castle of Sant' Angelo. Now he has escaped.

Outside they hear Tosca calling, "Mario!"

Cavaradossi gives his friend the basket of food and sends him back into the chapel.

Tosca is annoyed because Cavaradossi has kept her waiting. When he opens the door for her, she asks if he is hiding someone from her.

"Never!" he answers.

She tells him she hopes to meet him that evening. Tosca is a singer. She is singing tonight, but after the performance they can be together.

He replies that he will meet her. Then, thinking of Angelotti, he suggests that she leave him to his work.

Tosca is not used to being dismissed. Wounded and angry, she starts to go, then stops, her eyes on the picture he is painting.

"Who is that blonde woman?" she asks. Looking closely, she recognizes the face. "The Attavani woman!" she cries. "She has come here? She loves you? You love her?"

Cavaradossi explains that he saw the woman only by chance and painted the picture unknown to her.

"Swear it!" she demands, and he swears.

Reassured, she goes away.

Angelotti comes out of the Attavani chapel. Now Cavaradossi understands that the beautiful blonde woman who comes to pray is Angelotti's sister.

"She placed a woman's costume for me there under the altar, complete with scarf, veil, and fan," says Angelotti. In this disguise he hopes to escape from Scarpia, the feared and hated chief of the Roman police.

Cavaradossi offers his villa as a hiding place.

Angelotti takes the bundle of clothing from under the altar. "Shall I wear it?" he asks. Cavaradossi tells him it will not be necessary. The path to the villa is deserted.

They hear a cannon shot. It is the signal that Angelotti's escape has been discovered.

They hurry out together.

The sacristan returns with the latest news of the war. Napoleon's army has been crushed, he shouts. He calls the priests, choirboys, and others connected with the church and tells them they will all take part in a grand victory celebration that night.

"We'll be paid double wages—long live the king!" shout the choirboys, and they pay no attention to the sacristan, who is trying to quiet them.

A forbidding-looking figure appears in the doorway. It is Scarpia. With him are Spoletta and several other police agents.

The unruly boys creep silently out. The sacristan starts to follow them. Scarpia calls him back.

"A prisoner has escaped," says the chief. "He took refuge in this church and may still be here. Where is the Attavani chapel?"

The sacristan shows him the chapel. The gate is unlocked and open. Scarpia searches the chapel but finds only a fan—part of the disguise left by Angelotti's sister.

From the coat of arms on the fan he recognizes it as belonging to the Marchesa Attavani. He looks at the painting and sees that it is a portrait of the marchesa.

"Who is the painter?" he asks.

"Cavaradossi," answers the sacristan.

Scarpia knows Cavaradossi not only as Tosca's lover, but as a political enemy. He suspects the artist has helped Angelotti escape.

One of the police agents finds the empty lunch basket in the chapel.

The sacristan stares at it in astonishment. A short while ago the basket was full, he says. Cavaradossi surely did not eat the food; he was not hungry. Besides, he could not have left the basket in the chapel, since he had no key to the gate.

Now all is clear to Scarpia.

Tosca returns to the church. She has another message for Cavaradossi. Because she must sing at the victory celebration, she cannot meet him that evening.

Scarpia steps out of sight as she calls impatiently, "Mario, Mario!"

The sacristan tells her the painter has disappeared. She begins to doubt again, wondering if Mario is deceiving her.

Scarpia is watching from behind a pillar. For a long time he has loved Tosca. Now he sees a way to play on her jealousy, a chance of separating her and Cavaradossi.

He appears and piously offers her holy water. He shows her the fan he has found.

"Where did you find it?" she asks.

"It was near the easel," he says.

Tosca examines the fan and finds it belongs to the Marchesa Attavani.

"It is all as I suspected!" she cries. She is sure Mario and the blonde woman are together in his villa. She hurries off to surprise them.

Scarpia orders Spoletta to have her followed.

A crowd has gathered, waiting for the cardinal, who comes into the church and blesses the throng. During the singing of the *Te Deum,* Scarpia is lost in his own thoughts. He has two goals, both of them in sight. One is to see Cavaradossi hanged. The other is to possess the beautiful Tosca.

Act II shows Scarpia's apartment in the palace. Scarpia is at the table, having supper alone.

The Queen of Naples is giving a victory ball in the palace. Tosca will be there to sing in the cantata.

Scarpia calls Sciarrone, a policeman, and instructs him to meet her and bring her here after she has sung.

Spoletta arrives and reports the happenings of the afternoon. He followed Tosca to Cavaradossi's villa. She went inside and left soon afterward. He and his men went into the house. Cavaradossi was there, but they could find no trace of Angelotti.

The painter was so defiant, says Spoletta, that they thought it best to arrest him.

Scarpia sends for the prisoner, along with a judge, the executioner, and police agents.

Cavaradossi is brought in. Haughtily he demands to know why he has been arrested.

While Scarpia questions him, they hear the music of the cantata and the voice of Tosca.

"Where is Angelotti?" asks Scarpia.

"I do not know," answers Cavaradossi.

Time after time he refuses to confess.

Tosca enters. "Mario, why are you here?" she asks in astonishment.

He tells her under his breath, "Say nothing of what you saw!"

The judge, the executioner, and the police officers take Cavaradossi into the next room. Scarpia invites Tosca to sit down for a friendly talk. He speaks of the fan.

Tosca answers that she was foolish to be upset over such a trifle.

Scarpia asks if she found the Attavani woman at the villa.

She replies that no one was there except Cavaradossi.

Sciarrone comes to the door. He reports that the prisoner still refuses to confess.

"You must insist," Scarpia tells him.

"It is useless," says Tosca, and Scarpia answers, "We shall see." He tells her bluntly that the next room is a torture chamber.

She hears Cavaradossi cry out in pain.

"You can save him," says Scarpia.

She begs that the torture be stopped. Scarpia gives the order for the prisoner to be untied.

She calls to Cavaradossi. He answers in a faint voice, again telling her to say nothing.

"Speak, Tosca," says Scarpia.

"I know nothing," she answers.

Scarpia tells Spoletta to open the door wider so that she may hear Mario's moans of pain.

She can bear no more. She reveals the secret. Angelotti is hiding in the well in Mario's garden.

The torture is ceased. The police agents carry Cavaradossi into the room and put him down on the sofa. He has fainted. Tosca kneels and takes him in her arms.

He revives and hears Scarpia say to Spoletta, "The well in the garden—go!"

Cavaradossi knows then that Tosca has told the secret. "You've betrayed me!" he says, and he pushes her away from him.

Sciarrone brings news of the war. The earlier report was false. Napoleon's army has not been crushed. It has conquered, and the Roman troops are in flight.

To Mario this means that the Roman republic will be restored. He leaps to his feet, shouting, "Victory!"

Scarpia listens cynically to Cavaradossi's outpouring of defiance. Then he tells him that he is to be hanged.

Tosca tries to cling to Cavaradossi, but he is dragged away and she is forced back into the room. Again she and Scarpia are alone.

He invites her to sit down at the table with him. Perhaps, he says, they can find some way of saving Mario.

In a voice of utter contempt she asks, "What is your price?"

The price, he answers, is herself.

From outside the palace they hear drums—beating, he tells her, for those about to die. The last hour of Mario's life is near.

Tosca cries despairingly that she has lived for love and art, she has prayed, she has harmed no one. Why, then, has heaven forsaken her now?

Scarpia tells her coldly to make her decision.

Spoletta brings word that Angelotti was trapped and committed suicide.

"What of the other prisoner?" asks Scarpia.

Spoletta answers that all is ready for the execution.

Scarpia turns to Tosca and asks her softly if she agrees to his terms. Weeping, she nods her head. She asks that Cavaradossi be freed at once.

This cannot be done, he says. It must be arranged so that the public will think the execution has taken place.

He gives the order to Spoletta. The sentence has been changed. Cavaradossi will be shot, but it will be a mock execution. He adds with emphasis, "It will be the same as with Count Palmieri."

"I understand," answers Spoletta.

Tosca asks if she may tell Mario herself. Scarpia tells Spoletta to admit her to the prison early in the morning.

Spoletta leaves.

"I've kept my promise," says Scarpia.

But she and Mario will need a safe-conduct, she says, so that they may leave Rome together.

He goes to his desk. While he is writing, she sees a knife on the table. She picks it up and hides it behind her.

He finishes writing the safe-conduct. He goes to Tosca. "At last you are mine!" he says.

As he tries to take her in his arms, she stabs him in the heart.

He staggers and falls. He begs for help. She heaps insults on him as he dies.

She takes the safe-conduct from his clenched fist. Looking down on him, she speaks. "And before him all Rome trembled!"

Now that he is dead, she forgives him. She takes two lighted candles and places them on either side of his head. She lays a crucifix on his breast and hurries from the room.

Act III takes place on a platform high in the fortress of Sant' Angelo. To the left is a low wall. To the right is the head of a staircase. In the background are the Vatican and St. Peter's Cathedral. Stars are shining in the gray light just before dawn.

Far below a shepherd boy is singing.

Soldiers lead Cavaradossi up onto the platform and leave him with the jailer.

"You have one hour left," says the jailer.

Sitting at the table on the platform, Cavaradossi begins a letter of farewell to Tosca, but after a few lines he pauses, thinking of the happiness he has known with her. Never before has life meant so much, and now he must die.

Spoletta comes up the stairs. Behind him is Tosca. She goes to Cavaradossi and hands him the safe-conduct.

He is incredulous. This is the first time, he says, that Scarpia has ever shown mercy.

"And the last time," says Tosca. Speaking so the guard cannot hear, she tells him she has killed Scarpia. She has brought money and jewels, and a carriage is waiting to take them away from Rome. There will be a mock execution. At the sound of the shot he must fall. The soldiers will leave. "Then," she says, "we will go to the seacoast, board a ship, and be off to sea!"

The firing squad enters. Tosca cautions him to play his part well and be sure to fall at the first shot.

Cavaradossi stands against the wall. The soldiers fire, and he falls.

She watches anxiously, afraid he may speak or move too soon. The soldiers leave. She goes to him.

"Quick, Mario," she says.

He does not move. She touches him. Scarpia has deceived her. Cavaradossi is dead.

Excited voices come from below. Scarpia's murder has been discovered. The police are seeking Tosca.

Spoletta comes up the stairs. "You shall pay for his life!" he cries.

Before he can seize her, she thrusts him back. She springs to the top of the low wall and leaps to her death. Soldiers come onto the platform and look down after her, while Spoletta stands gazing in horror.

# Madame Butterfly

In 1900 one of the popular Broadway plays was *Madame Butterfly*, written by David Belasco and based on a story by John Luther Long. The same year the play was taken to London. Puccini saw it there and made plans to set the story to music.

His opera was first performed in Milan on February 17, 1904. It was a total failure.

Puccini rewrote the score. The second performance, in Brescia on May 28, 1904, was a success.

*Madame Butterfly* takes place in Japan early in the twentieth century. The setting is a house with a terrace and garden high on a hill overlooking Nagasaki.

Goro, a marriage broker, and Lieutenant B. F. Pinkerton of the United States Navy, are on the terrace. The young American has just taken the house for himself and his Japanese bride.

Besides arranging the marriage and locating the house, the marriage broker has also provided three servants. One of them he introduces as Suzuki, who will be the maid-servant of Pinkerton's bride.

Sharpless, the United States consul, arrives for the wedding. He and Pinkerton wait in the garden for the other guests. The lieutenant talks of the beauty and charm of the girl he has chosen. Her name is Cho-Cho-San, but she is known as Butterfly.

Sharpless knows how little the marriage means to the young man and how much it means to the girl. He warns Pinkerton against the step he is about to take.

Pinkerton only laughs and lifts his glass in a toast to the day when he is really married to an American wife.

Butterfly and a party of women come up the hill and into the garden. With great ceremony she introduces Pinkerton.

Sharpless speaks to her kindly and she tells him about herself. Her family was once wealthy. When their wealth was gone, she became a public entertainer—a geisha—to earn her living. Her age is fifteen. She says, "I am old, am I not?"

Her relations begin to arrive. The imperial commissioner and the official registrar take their places.

Butterfly shows Pinkerton her sleeves stuffed with possessions she has brought from home. She takes out handkerchiefs, a few trinkets, and a knife in a sheath.

The knife is sacred, she says.

Goro whispers to Pinkerton that the emperor of Japan sent the knife to her father, who obediently committed suicide with it.

Butterfly tells Pinkerton that she has given up the religion of her ancestors. From now on she will worship as he does.

The commissioner reads the marriage contract, and it is signed. The bride's friends crowd about her, addressing her as Madame Butterfly.

"No," she corrects them. "Madame B. F. Pinkerton."

Sharpless and the other officials leave. While Pinkerton is wondering how to get rid of the other wedding guests, Butterfly's uncle comes storming into the garden. He knows that Butterfly has turned from her religion.

"You have renounced us all!" he cries, and some of the other relatives turn on her, crying, "And we renounce you!"

Pinkerton orders them all to go, and they leave, shouting curses as they file down the hill.

Butterfly is weeping. Pinkerton comforts her.

Night falls. They watch the stars for a while, then they go into the house together.

The scene of Act II is Butterfly's house. The time is three years later.

Suzuki is praying before the image of Buddha. Butterfly asks her, "How soon shall we be starving?"

The maid goes to a cabinet and takes out the few coins that are left. Unless Lieutenant Pinkerton comes back quickly, she says, the situation is desperate.

He will come back, says Butterfly.

"I never knew of a foreign husband who did," says Suzuki.

Butterfly repeats what Pinkerton promised before he went away: "I'll come back when the robins are nesting."

She tells the maid how it will be. One fine day they will see a thread of smoke rising out at sea, and his ship will come in sight. It will sail into the harbor. A man will come from the city, a speck in the distance, climbing the hill. When he reaches the top, he will call, "Butterfly!" and she will be in Pinkerton's arms again.

Suzuki is not convinced. Butterfly sends her away.

Goro and Sharpless come into the garden. The marriage broker stays outside, and the consul calls on Butterfly.

He has brought news of Pinkerton, but before he can deliver it, she asks a question. At what time of the year do robins build their nests in America?

"Why?" asks Sharpless.

"My husband promised to come back in the season when robins build their nests," she answers. "Here they have built them three times already. I thought that there they might not build so often."

Goro has been listening outside. He laughs out loud.

She turns and sees him. He comes forward and bows.

She tells the consul, "He is a wicked fellow. B. F. Pinkerton was hardly gone before this man came here urging me to marry again. Now—"

Goro intervenes. Now, he says, he wants her to marry Prince Yamadori, a wealthy man.

The prince comes to the door, followed by two servants carrying flowers. Butterfly greets him with scorn. She is not interested in him, she says. She has a husband already.

Yamadori goes sadly away. Goro goes with him.

Sharpless tries to prepare Butterfly for the news he has brought—that Pinkerton will soon be back in Nagasaki, but does not want to see her again.

"What would you do," he begins, "if he were never to come back?"

She answers that she might become an entertainer again—either that, or die.

Sharpless gently tries to persuade her to marry Prince Yamadori. She is shocked. Does he think Pinkerton has forgotten his love for her?

She runs out of the room and comes back with a child in her arms. "Look! Could such as *he* be forgotten?"

Sharpless is startled. He asks, "Does Pinkerton know he has a son?"

"No," she answers. The child was born while his father was far away. She asks Sharpless to write to Pinkerton and tell him of the fine son waiting for him. Then he will surely come back.

The child's name is Trouble, she says. On the day of Pinkerton's return the name shall be changed to Joy.

The consul cannot bear to tell Butterfly the news he has brought. He leaves, after promising that Pinkerton shall be told of his child.

Suzuki catches Goro still skulking about. She drags him into the house. Butterfly threatens his life with her father's dagger and drives him away.

There is a cannon shot in the harbor—the signal that a ship is coming into port. Butterfly takes a telescope and goes out upon the terrace. She reads the name of the ship: "Abraham Lincoln."

It is Pinkerton's ship!

"Now do you see how foolish it is to doubt?" she cries.

She and Suzuki decorate the house with flowers. Butterfly puts on her wedding robe, and Suzuki dresses the baby. Butterfly makes three small holes in the screen so they may each look out toward the harbor to watch for Pinkerton.

The house grows dark. The baby sinks down on his cushion and falls asleep. Suzuki, crouching beside him, falls asleep, too. Only Butterfly remains at her post.

The closing scene takes place the following morning. Suzuki and the child are still sleeping. Butterfly is still looking out through the screen.

Suzuki wakes. She persuades Butterfly to rest. "When he is here, I will call you," she says.

Butterfly takes the child and goes away.

Sharpless and Pinkerton come to the door, and Suzuki lets them in. She tells Pinkerton how Butterfly has waited. "I'll call her," she says, and Pinkerton says, "Not yet."

She sees a strange American woman in the garden.

"Who is that?" she asks.

It is Sharpless who answers. The woman is Pinkerton's wife.

Suzuki breaks into a wild lament. Sharpless quiets her. They must think of the child's future, he says. The lady outside will take the baby and give him a mother's care.

Pinkerton sees the flowers that have been brought to honor his coming. He sees his own picture in a prominent place, and he is filled with shame. He had not realized that Butterfly would remain faithful.

Unable to face the situation, he goes away.

Suzuki brings Kate Pinkerton in from the garden.

Butterfly has heard voices. She comes running into the room. Seeing the consul, she thinks Pinkerton, too, must be there. Excitedly she looks for him.

She sees Kate Pinkerton.

"Who is this woman?" she asks.

No one answers.

She asks Suzuki, "Why are you weeping?"

Still no one answers, but now Butterfly has begun to understand.

"He will come to me no more," she says.

Kate asks if Pinkerton may have his son.

Yes, says Butterfly, if he will climb the hill half an hour from now.

Sharpless takes Kate Pinkerton away.

Butterfly orders Suzuki to darken the room. The maid closes the door and covers the windows.

"Where is the child?" asks Butterfly.

"At play," says Suzuki.

"Go and play with him," says Butterfly, and Suzuki goes.

Butterfly lights the lamp before the image of Buddha. She takes the knife from the wall and reads the words written on the blade: "Death with honor is better than life with dishonor."

Suzuki pushes the child into the room. Butterfly catches him in her arms and bids him farewell. She gives him a small American flag and a doll, turns his face from her, and gently bandages his eyes.

With the knife in her hand, she goes behind a screen.

There is a silence. The knife falls heavily to the floor. Butterfly comes from behind the screen with a white veil wrapped about her throat. She drags herself toward the child.

From outside, Pinkerton calls, "Butterfly!"

He and Sharpless burst into the room. Butterfly points to the child and dies. Sobbing, Pinkerton drops to his knees beside her, while Sharpless takes the child in his arms.

# Der Rosenkavalier

With two grim operas behind him—*Elektra* and *Salome* —the German composer Richard Strauss turned to a happier subject. This was *Der Rosenkavalier* ("The Cavalier of the Rose"), a comedy of eighteenth-century Vienna.

The opera was begun in the spring of 1909 and the score was finished toward the close of the following year. It was first performed in Dresden on January 26, 1911.

The scene of Act I is the apartment of Princess von Werdenberg. It is early morning. The princess is lying on a couch. Octavian, a youth of a noble family, is kneeling before her.

He is jealous of the day, he declares, because in the daytime all men may look upon her. He springs up and draws the window curtains, shutting out the light, and she smiles in tender amusement.

A little black boy comes into the room. He is hung with silver bells that tinkle as he moves. He has brought the princess' morning chocolate.

While the princess and Octavian have breakfast, they hear someone coming up the private staircase. The princess' husband is away on a hunting expedition. They are afraid he has returned.

She listens to the voices outside. It is not her husband, she says. It is her cousin, Baron Ochs.

She tells Octavian to hide until her visitor leaves.

Octavian goes out and returns dressed as a lady's maid. They laugh at his disguise. On his way back into the next room he bumps into the baron, who has just entered.

As much as the princess dislikes her cousin's grossness and vulgarity, she is gracious toward him.

He is looking at Octavian with interest.

The princess explains that this is her new maid just arrived from the country. "I am afraid her rough manners have displeased you."

"On the contrary," says the baron. "I like such manners."

He tells the princess why he has come. He has decided to marry young Sophie Faninal. Her family has lately been raised to the rank of nobility. The girl is pretty and her father is wealthy, and the baron thinks it will be an ideal match.

He wishes to give the bride a silver rose as a pledge of his love. Among the nobility it is the custom for this gift to be presented by someone of noble birth. Baron Ochs wants the princess to help him choose a rose-bearer for this important ceremony.

She asks the supposed maid, whom she calls Mariandel, to bring a certain jeweled miniature. Octavian brings it. It is a picture of Octavian himself.

The princess shows it to the baron. "Do you wish this young man to deliver the silver rose?" she asks.

The baron answers that he would be honored. Looking from the picture to the supposed maid, he remarks that they look amazingly alike.

It is time for the princess to receive the various people who have gathered outside. Her lawyer is there, and there are the usual favor-seekers—a milliner, a scholar, an animal vendor with little dogs and an ape, a mother with three daughters, a tenor with an Italian song to sing, a flute-player, and a furtive-looking couple named Valzacchi and Annina, who have the latest scandal for sale.

The hairdresser arrives with his assistant. While the princess' hair is being arranged, she tries to give her attention to the group about her. She is gracious to all except Valzacchi and Annina. She tells them shortly that she has no interest in their vulgar scandal.

Baron Ochs talks with the princess' lawyer. He thinks if he honors Sophie Faninal by marrying her, he should be made heir to the Faninal estate. The lawyer tells him the law makes no such provision. The baron beats angrily on the table, and the lawyer retreats in alarm.

Valzacchi and Annina approach the baron. They offer to spy on his young bride and report to him every step she takes.

He asks them if they can tell him anything about the princess' maid, Mariandel. They are completely baffled, but they assure him they will soon have the information he wants.

The baron's servants bring the jewel case in which is the silver rose. The princess promises that the Count Octavian will present it, and she dismisses the baron.

She thinks with pity of the young bride he will soon be taking. "Once I was such a bride," she reflects, "and now, before long, I shall be known as the old princess."

Octavian returns. Again he declares his love for her. She tells him quietly that some day he will leave her, and she sends him away.

But when he has gone, she tries to call him back. She sends her footmen after him, but they are too late. The young man has already ridden off.

She calls the little black boy and gives him the jewel case left by Baron Ochs. "Carry it to Count Octavian," she says, "and tell him the silver rose is inside. He will understand."

The scene of Act II is the Faninal house. Faninal is

leaving. The rose-bearer is expected, and according to custom the father may not be present when the silver rose is delivered.

"But when I come back," Faninal promises his daughter, Sophie, "I shall be leading your bridegroom by the hand!"

He leaves, and Sophie begins to pray. It is a solemn day, and she thanks God for blessing her high above her worth.

Marianne, the woman who watches over her, is at the window, reporting excitedly on what is happening outside. People have gathered. Half the town is there. Now the bridegroom's messenger is arriving!

"God in heaven," prays Sophie, "I know that pride is a sin, but today I cannot be humble—it is all so beautiful!"

Octavian enters, accompanied by his attendants. He is splendidly dressed in silver and white. Sophie is awed by his magnificence. He is overcome by her beauty.

He presents the rose. She accepts it. After the formal ceremony, the attendants go outside. Only Marianne is left with Sophie and Octavian.

More at ease now, Sophie talks about her coming marriage. She is glad she will be married soon—a girl is nothing until she has a man to guide her.

Octavian is deeply moved by her sweetness and innocence. "How fair and good she is!" he thinks.

Faninal returns, conducting the bridegroom, and

Sophie is presented to him. The baron pats her and says she is tender as a young chicken.

Marianne simpers delightedly at his free and easy manners. Faninal wishes the walls were made of glass so all the town could see a real nobleman paying court to his little daughter.

But Sophie shrinks from the baron's coarseness, and Octavian looks on in silent anger.

The lawyer enters. He and Faninal and the baron go to discuss the financial arrangements of the marriage.

Sophie is close to tears. Not for the world would she marry the baron, she says, and she appeals to Octavian for help.

"Take courage," he says. "You must strike a blow for us two."

"For us two?" she repeats.

He is in love with her, he says, and he promises that somehow he will save her. She answers that all her trust is placed in him.

Two figures creep into sight on opposite sides of the room. They are the scandalmongers, Valzacchi and Annina. They move forward, listening.

"I will follow wherever you guide me," says Sophie.

"My heart will be with you always," says Octavian.

The eavesdroppers come out of hiding. Valzacchi seizes Octavian. Annina seizes Sophie.

"Baron—Baron!" screams Annina.

"Come see your future bride with a young gentleman!" shouts Valzacchi.

The baron comes into the room. Far from being disturbed, he is amused at what he takes to be a harmless flirtation. He leads Sophie toward the next room to sign the marriage contract.

Octavian stops him. "The lady will have none of you," he says.

The baron tries to drag Sophie away.

Octavian draws his sword. The baron draws to defend himself, and Octavian wounds him in the arm.

"Murder! Help!" roars the baron. His servants close in around Octavian, who holds them off with his sword.

Faninal enters. Sophie tries to explain what has happened. "His lordship behaved dishonorably toward me," she says.

"Are you speaking of my future son-in-law?" returns her father indignantly.

She answers that she no longer looks on the baron as her future husband.

Faninal is in a rage. How can he face his neighbors if this marriage is broken off? He will be the laughingstock of the town.

"Before I marry him," says Sophie, "I'll lock myself in my room and starve."

He answers that he has men enough to break down the door and drag her to the coach.

"I'll jump out of the coach on the way to the church," she says.

"I'll sit by your side and hold you," he says.

"Then I'll say 'No' at the altar," she says.

"If you say 'No,' I'll send you to a convent!" he says fiercely, and he orders her out of his sight.

Marianne pushes Octavian out one door and leads Sophie away through another.

A doctor comes to attend the baron. Faninal leaves to have wine sent in.

The baron's pain and anger begin to subside. He recalls Sophie's defiance with a certain pleasure. He likes a girl with spirit.

Annina enters. She has a letter for him, and she reads it aloud: " 'Tomorrow evening I am free. I liked you, but felt ashamed to say it, for I am only a young thing. I await an answer.' " It is signed "Mariandel."

The baron is delighted at this show of interest from the princess' pretty maid. He tells Annina to come back later and he will give her an answer in writing.

Annina hints that she would like to be paid for her services. He ignores her, and she shakes her fist behind him in a way that suggests she will pay him back for his stinginess.

Act III takes place the next evening in a private room of an inn. Annina is there, dressed as a lady in mourning. Valzacchi is helping her complete her disguise.

Octavian enters. He, too, is disguised—as Mariandel, the princess' maid. His plan is to bring the baron here, thoroughly confuse him and place him in an embarrassing position, then expose him to Sophie's father.

Valzacchi and Annina are now employed by Octavian. Several men enter and receive instructions from Valzacchi. The instructions have to do with a trap door and secret panels in the wall.

Octavian brings Baron Ochs to the inn. The baron's personal servant is with them. The landlord and waiters shower their noble guest with attention. He gets rid of them all, and sits alone with the supposed Mariandel.

Again he is struck by Mariandel's resemblance to Octavian. He mutters that the face of that boy seems to pursue him.

Before he can recover from this unpleasantness, he sees a ghostly figure disappearing into the floor.

He fears his brain is becoming fevered, and he takes off his wig. As he does so, a face stares at him out of the wall and is gone in an instant.

Shock follows shock. Other ghostly faces peer out of the walls. A widow—Annina in disguise—enters and declares he is her husband who deserted her. Four children dance about him, crying, "Papa, papa!"

Baron Ochs flings open the window and calls the police.

A policeman arrives and questions the people in the

room. The baron cannot prove his identity, and his servant runs to bring help.

The policeman asks the baron, "Who is this girl with you?"

"She is Sophie Faninal, my bride-to-be," answers the baron.

Octavian's messengers have gone to bring Sophie's father.

Faninal enters.

"Who asked you to interfere?" says the baron.

Faninal replies that messengers called him to rescue the baron from grave danger.

The policeman questions Faninal. "This girl is your daughter?" he asks, pointing to Octavian.

"My daughter? That hussy!" says Faninal. He is further outraged at the sight of the disguised Annina and the four children, who are still shouting, "Papa, papa!"

Sophie has been waiting outside. Her father sends for her.

"There, see your noble bridegroom!" he exclaims, pointing to the sputtering baron who has lost his wig. "See him there with his wife and children. And that"—pointing to Octavian—"that is *you!*"

He almost chokes on the words. Faintness seizes him, and he has to be carried out. Sophie goes to help care for him.

The baron finds his wig and puts it on. Now some of

his dignity is restored. The policeman again asks him about the young woman at his table.

"I'll tell you later who she is," blusters the baron.

Octavian takes the policeman aside and reveals his identity. The policeman begins to laugh.

Octavian steps into an alcove. At the same time the Princess von Werdenberg is announced. The baron's servant has called her to come and help his master. She enters, with the little black boy carrying her train.

She waits for the situation to be explained to her.

Octavian comes out of the alcove. He has taken off his disguise. Sophie enters. She sees only the baron, and she tells him that all is over between them. Her father has forbidden him to come within a hundred yards of the Faninal house.

He starts toward the next room to speak with Faninal. Sophie runs out ahead of him and shuts the door in his face.

The princess touches his shoulder. She suggests that for the sake of his dignity he leave now.

Sophie returns. This time she sees the princess and Octavian.

The princess tells the policeman the whole incident has been a joke and nothing more. He bows respectfully and leaves.

The baron is eyeing Octavian. "That face. I'm sick of it!" he says. He is growing confused again.

The princess advises him not to think too much. She tells him he may as well give up all hope of any alliance with the Faninal family.

The hired conspirators come out of their hiding places. The landlord, waiters, musicians, and coachmen gather about the baron and ask to be paid for their services. He runs out, followed by the clamoring crowd.

Sophie, Octavian, and the princess are alone.

Sophie watches Octavian and the princess, their faces close together. She thinks, "It was all a game to him. I am nothing to him now."

But Octavian, hesitating and embarrassed, is trying to explain to the princess that he loves Sophie. He never meant to fall in love with the girl, he says. It happened without his willing it.

"Go to her," says the princess.

He goes to Sophie. "Have you no kindly word for me?" he asks.

She answers that she had hoped he would befriend her in quite a different way. She is rid of the baron, it is true, but now she is ashamed and she feels the princess is looking at her with pity and scorn. She starts to leave.

The princess leaves instead. She has known that some day she must give up Octavian, but, she tells herself with bitter sadness, she did not know it would be so soon.

Octavian takes Sophie in his arms.

Faninal and the princess come in together. Sophie's

father is happy again. The new arrangement pleases him. Not only that, the princess has invited the three of them to ride home in her carriage.

He and the princess leave. Octavian kisses Sophie. Unnoticed, her handkerchief falls. They follow Faninal and the princess.

For a few moments the room is empty. Then the little black boy returns. He looks for the handkerchief. He finds it. He picks it up and runs out, and the curtain quickly falls.

# CASTS OF CHARACTERS

## The Marriage of Figaro
by WOLFGANG AMADEUS MOZART

### CAST

Figaro ................................. *Baritone*
Susanna ................................ *Soprano*
Doctor Bartolo ............................ *Bass*
Marcellina ........................ *Mezzo-soprano*
Cherubino ............................. *Soprano*
Count Almaviva ........................ *Baritone*
Don Basilio ............................... *Tenor*
Countess Almaviva ...................... *Soprano*
Antonio .................................. *Bass*
Don Curzio ............................. *Tenor*
Barbarina ............................. *Soprano*

→→→←←←

## Don Giovanni
by WOLFGANG AMADEUS MOZART

### CAST

Leporello .................................. *Bass*
Don Giovanni ..................... *Baritone or bass*
Donna Anna ............................ *Soprano*
The Commandant .......................... *Bass*
Don Ottavio ............................. *Tenor*
Donna Elvira .......................... *Soprano*
Zerlina ................................. *Soprano*
Masetto ......................... *Baritone or bass*

259

## The Magic Flute
### by WOLFGANG AMADEUS MOZART

CAST

Tamino ................................. *Tenor*
Three ladies ................ *Sopranos and contralto*
Papageno ............................. *Baritone*
Queen of the Night ..................... *Soprano*
Monostatos ............................. *Tenor*
Pamina ................................. *Soprano*
Three spirits ............... *Sopranos and contralto*
A priest ................................. *Bass*
Two priests ................... *Tenor and baritone*
Sarastro ................................. *Bass*
Papagena ............................. *Soprano*

➤➤➤◄◄◄

## The Barber of Seville
### by GIOACCHINO ROSSINI

CAST

Count Almaviva .......................... *Tenor*
Fiorello ................................. *Bass*
Figaro ................................. *Baritone*
Rosina ................................. *Soprano*
Doctor Bartolo ........................... *Bass*
Don Basilio ............................. *Bass*
Berta ............................ *Mezzo-soprano*
Ambrogio ............................. *Bass*

## *Lucia di Lammermoor*
### by GAETANO DONIZETTI

#### CAST

| | |
|---|---|
| Normanno | Tenor |
| Enrico Ashton | Baritone |
| Raimondo Bidebent | Bass |
| Lucia | Soprano |
| Alisa | Mezzo-soprano |
| Edgardo | Tenor |
| Arturo Bucklaw | Tenor |

→→><←←←

## *Tannhauser*
### by RICHARD WAGNER

#### CAST

| | | |
|---|---|---|
| Tannhauser | | Tenor |
| Venus | | Soprano |
| A shepherd | | Soprano |
| The landgrave | | Bass |
| Wolfram | | Baritone |
| Walther | | Tenor |
| Biterolf | Minstrel knights | Bass |
| Heinrich | | Tenor |
| Reinmar | | Bass |
| Elisabeth | | Soprano |

## Lohengrin
### by Richard Wagner

C A S T

King Henry ............................... *Bass*
Telramund ............................ *Baritone*
A herald .................................. *Bass*
Ortrud ........................... *Mezzo-soprano*
Elsa .................................. *Soprano*
Lohengrin .............................. *Tenor*
Gottfried

>>>><<<

## Tristan and Isolde
### by Richard Wagner

C A S T

A sailor ................................. *Tenor*
Isolde .................................. *Soprano*
Brangaene ............................. *Soprano*
Tristan ................................. *Tenor*
Kurvenal .............................. *Baritone*
Melot .................................. *Tenor*
King Mark .............................. *Bass*
A shepherd ............................. *Tenor*
A helmsman ........................... *Baritone*

>>>><<<

## The Mastersingers of Nuremberg
### by RICHARD WAGNER

CAST

| | | |
|---|---|---|
| Walther | ............................... | *Tenor* |
| Eva | ................................... | *Soprano* |
| Magdalena | ............................ | *Soprano* |
| David | ................................. | *Tenor* |
| Pogner | ......... | ............ *Bass* |
| Beckmesser | ....... | ............ *Bass* |
| Hans Sachs | ...... | ............ *Bass* |
| Vogelsang | ....... | ............ *Tenor* |
| Nachtigal | ........ | ............ *Bass* |
| Kothner | ......... | ............ *Bass* |
| Zorn | ............ | ............ *Tenor* |
| Eisslinger | ....... | ............ *Tenor* |
| Moser | .......... | ............ *Tenor* |
| Ortel | ........... | ............ *Bass* |
| Schwartz | ........ | ............ *Bass* |
| Foltz | ........... | ............ *Bass* |
| A nightwatchman | ........................... | *Bass* |

(braced together as } Mastersingers {)

>>>><<<<

## Parsifal
### by RICHARD WAGNER

CAST

| | | |
|---|---|---|
| Gurnemanz | .............................. | *Bass* |
| Kundry | ................................ | *Soprano* |
| Amfortas | .............................. | *Baritone* |
| Parsifal | ................................. | *Tenor* |
| Four esquires | .................. | *Sopranos and tenors* |
| Two knights of the Grail | ............. | *Tenor and bass* |
| Titurel | ................................. | *Bass* |
| Klingsor | ................................ | *Bass* |

## Rigoletto
### by Giuseppe Verdi

CAST

| | |
|---|---|
| The Duke of Mantua | *Tenor* |
| Borsa | *Tenor* |
| Rigoletto | *Baritone* |
| Countess Ceprano | *Mezzo-soprano* |
| Count Ceprano | *Bass* |
| Marullo | *Baritone* |
| Count Monterone | *Baritone* |
| Sparafucile | *Bass* |
| Gilda | *Soprano* |
| Giovanna | *Mezzo-soprano* |
| Maddalena | *Contralto* |

→→)(←←

## Il Trovatore
### by Giuseppe Verdi

CAST

| | |
|---|---|
| Ferrando | *Bass* |
| Leonora | *Soprano* |
| Inez | *Soprano* |
| Count di Luna | *Baritone* |
| Manrico | *Tenor* |
| Azucena | *Mezzo-soprano* |
| Ruiz | *Tenor* |

## La Traviata
### by GIUSEPPE VERDI

CAST

Violetta ................................. *Soprano*
Flora ............................ *Mezzo-soprano*
Baron Duphol .......................... *Baritone*
Doctor Grenvil ............................ *Bass*
Marquis d'Obigny ......................... *Bass*
Gastone ................................. *Tenor*
Alfredo ................................. *Tenor*
Annina ................................. *Soprano*
Germont .............................. *Baritone*

➤➤➤◄◄◄

## Aida
### by GIUSEPPE VERDI

CAST

Radames ................................. *Tenor*
Ramphis ................................. *Bass*
Amneris ........................ *Mezzo-soprano*
Aida ................................. *Soprano*
The king ................................. *Bass*
Amonasro ............................. *Baritone*
A messenger ............................. *Tenor*
A priestess ............................. *Soprano*

## Faust
### by CHARLES GOUNOD

CAST

Faust ..................................... *Tenor*
Mephistopheles ..................... *Bass-baritone*
Valentine ............................. *Baritone*
Wagner ................................ *Baritone*
Siebel ........................... *Mezzo-soprano*
Marguerite ........................... *Soprano*
Martha .............................. *Contralto*

→→>←←←

## Carmen
### by GEORGES BIZET

CAST

Morales ................................ *Baritone*
Micaela ............................... *Soprano*
Don José ............................... *Tenor*
Zuniga ................................. *Bass*
Carmen ......................... *Mezzo-soprano*
Frasquita ............................. *Soprano*
Mercédès ............................. *Soprano*
Dancairo .............................. *Tenor*
Remendado ............................. *Tenor*
Escamillo ............................. *Baritone*

## Manon
### by Jules Massenet

CAST

Poussette ............................... *Soprano*
Javotte ................................. *Soprano*
Rosette ................................ *Soprano*
Guillot ................................... *Bass*
Bretigny ............................... *Baritone*
Manon ................................. *Soprano*
Lescaut ................................ *Baritone*
Chevalier Des Grieux ..................... *Tenor*
An innkeeper .............................. *Bass*
Count Des Grieux ......................... *Bass*

>>><<<

## Cavalleria Rusticana
### by Pietro Mascagni

CAST

Turiddu .................................. *Tenor*
Santuzza ............................... *Soprano*
Mamma Lucia ......................... *Contralto*
Alfio .................................. *Baritone*
Lola ............................. *Mezzo-soprano*

## I Pagliacci
### by RUGGIERO LEONCAVALLO

CAST

Tonio .................................. *Baritone*
Beppe ................................. *Tenor*
Canio ................................. *Tenor*
Nedda ................................ *Soprano*
Silvio ................................ *Baritone*

→→⤜←←

## La Bohème
### by GIACOMO PUCCINI

CAST

Rodolfo ............................... *Tenor*
Marcello .............................. *Baritone*
Colline ............................... *Bass*
Schaunard ............................ *Baritone*
Benoit ................................ *Bass*
Mimi ................................. *Soprano*
Parpignol, the vendor ................. *Tenor*
Musetta .............................. *Soprano*
Alcindoro ............................ *Bass*

→→⤜←←

## *Tosca*
### by GIACOMO PUCCINI

CAST

Angelotti ................................. *Bass*
A sacristan .............................. *Baritone*
Mario Cavaradossi ......................... *Tenor*
Tosca ................................... *Soprano*
Scarpia ................................. *Baritone*
Sciarrone ................................ *Bass*
Spoletta ................................ *Tenor*
A shepherd ............................. *Contralto*
A jailer ................................. *Bass*

>>>×<<<

## *Madame Butterfly*
### by GIACOMO PUCCINI

CAST

Goro ...................................... *Tenor*
B. F. Pinkerton .......................... *Tenor*
Sharpless ............................... *Baritone*
Suzuki ............................. *Mezzo-soprano*
Butterfly ............................... *Soprano*
The mother ............................. *Soprano*
The aunt ............................... *Soprano*
The cousin ............................. *Soprano*
The first uncle, Yakuside ................. *Baritone*
The imperial commissioner ................. *Bass*
The official registrar .................... *Baritone*
The second uncle, a Buddhist priest ........... *Bass*
Prince Yamadori ........................ *Baritone*
Kate Pinkerton .................... *Mezzo-soprano*
The child

## Der Rosenkavalier
### by RICHARD STRAUSS

CAST

Princess von Werdenberg .................. *Soprano*
Octavian .......................... *Mezzo-soprano*
Baron Ochs ................................ *Bass*
A lawyer ................................. *Bass*
A milliner .............................. *Soprano*
An animal vendor ......................... *Tenor*
A scholar
A hairdresser and his assistant
A flute player
A cook
A mother
Her three daughters .......... *Sopranos and contralto*
A singer ................................. *Tenor*
Valzacchi ................................ *Tenor*
Annina ............................... *Contralto*
Faninal .............................. *Baritone*
Sophie Faninal ......................... *Soprano*
Marianne ............................... *Soprano*
An innkeeper ............................ *Tenor*
A policeman ............................... *Bass*
Four children
Leopold, Baron Ochs' servant
A little black boy

➤➤➤◄◄◄

# BIOGRAPHICAL NOTES

Wolfgang Amadeus Mozart was born in Salzburg, Austria, on January 27, 1756. At the age of four he was a skilled pianist and had already begun to compose, and when he was six he began a series of concert tours that brought him fame throughout most of Europe. When he was a young man he settled in Vienna, where he composed most of his important works. He died there on December 5, 1791.

Gioacchino Rossini was born in Pesaro, Italy, on February 29, 1792. He studied music at the Bologna Conservatory, and he lived and worked in Italy, Austria, France, and England. After 1829 he composed no more operas. He died in Passy, near Paris, on November 13, 1868.

Gaetano Donizetti was born in Bergamo, Italy, on November 29, 1797. As a young man, he served in the army; and, while stationed in Venice, he composed his first operas. Most of his life he lived and worked in Italy. He died in Bergamo on April 8, 1848.

Richard Wagner was born in Leipzig, Germany, on May 22, 1813. In his early twenties he conducted for German opera companies and composed his first operas. From 1839 to 1842 he lived in London and Paris. In 1842 he returned to Germany and continued composing and conducting. He fled Germany in 1849 to avoid arrest for his part in an unsuccessful revolt against the government. During most of his exile he lived in Switzerland. In 1860 he was allowed to return to Germany. Wagner's last years were spent at Bayreuth, Germany, where he founded the Festival Theater. He died on February 13, 1883, during a visit to Venice.

GIUSEPPE VERDI was born in Roncole, Italy, on October 10, 1813. He studied music in Milan. His first opera was produced in 1839, his last in 1893. He cared little for travel and spent most of his life in his native country. He died in Milan on January 27, 1901.

CHARLES GOUNOD was born in Paris on June 17, 1818. He studied music in Paris and later in Rome. His first opera was given in Paris in 1851. In 1870 he went to England and lived there until 1874, when he returned to France. He died on October 18, 1893, at Saint-Cloud, France.

GEORGES BIZET was born in Paris on October 25, 1838. When he was nine he entered the Paris Conservatory, and when he was nineteen he went to Italy for several years' musical study. Back in Paris, he wrote much music, including several operas. He died in Bougival, France, on June 3, 1875.

JULES MASSENET was born in Montaud, France, on May 12, 1842. He studied music in Paris and Rome. After serving in the Franco-Prussian War, he continued composing and teaching composition until his death in Paris on August 13, 1912.

PIETRO MASCAGNI was born in Leghorn, Italy, on December 7, 1863. He left the Milan Conservatory to conduct a touring opera company. Later he taught music in southern Italy. In 1890 the production of his opera *Cavalleria Rusticana* brought him fame. He died in Rome on August 2, 1945.

RUGGIERO LEONCAVALLO was born in Naples on March 8, 1858. He was a student at the Naples Conservatory. Before the success of his opera *I Pagliacci*, he earned a living as a traveling musician. He died in Montecatini, Italy, on August 9, 1919.

GIACOMO PUCCINI was born in Lucca, Italy, on December 22, 1858. He was a student at the Milan Conservatory. Almost all his compositions were operas. He died in Brussels on November 29, 1924.

RICHARD STRAUSS was born in Munich on June 11, 1864. He studied music in Munich and grew up surrounded by the musical life of the city. He composed songs and symphonic works, as well as operas; and he served as musical director for several German theaters. He died in Garmisch, Germany, on September 8, 1949.

# INDEX

## ABOUT THE AUTHOR

CLYDE ROBERT BULLA was born near King City, Missouri. His formal education began in a one-room schoolhouse, where he wrote his first stories and composed his first songs.

Music, and opera in particular, has always been an important part of Mr. Bulla's life. He saw the need for a book which would tell the stories of the well-known operas in a simple and direct manner. The happy result —*Stories of Favorite Operas.*